From
the Angel's
Blackboard

From the Angel's Blackboard

──── *The Best of* ────
FULTON J. SHEEN

LIGUORI/TRIUMPH
LIGUORI, MISSOURI

Published by Liguori/Triumph
An Imprint of Liguori Publications
Liguori, Missouri
www.liguori.org

Library of Congress Cataloging-in-Publication Data

Sheen, Fulton J. (Fulton John), 1895–1979.
From the angel's blackboard : the best of Fulton J. Sheen.
p. cm.
Includes bibliographical references and index.
ISBN   0-89243-777-4, ISBN 0-89243-925-4 (pbk)
1. Christian life—Catholic authors. I. Title.
BX2350.2.S438   1995
248.4'82—dc20   94-42258

"Fingers, Hands, and Nails" is reprinted from *Life of Christ* by Fulton J. Sheen, © 1958, 1977, by Doubleday/Image, a Division of Bantam Doubleday Dell Publishing Group, Inc. Used with permission of publisher.

"Love's Overflow," from *The Divine Romance*, is reprinted with permission of Alba House.

Printed in the United States of America

First paperback edition 1996
05   7 6 5

Contents

HEART

SPIRIT

Editor's Foreword

A voice is silent in the midst of the Church and in our land, the like of which will not be heard again in our day . . .

Words that opened an unforgettable eulogy on December 13, 1979. Words that still echo through the years with a ring of truth.

Archbishop Fulton J. Sheen — charismatic prelate, powerful orator and thinker, popular television personality, and prolific writer of books as well as news columns for both the secular and religious press — was undoubtedly one of the best-loved religious figures of this century. And such was the tenacity of Sheen's mind, heart, and spirit that his greatest gift and legacy remain an indelible impact on the mind, heart, and spirit of all who call themselves God's people.

It is fitting, then, to mark the 100th anniversary of his birth with this special commemorative volume. In rereading many of Sheen's works, it becomes readily apparent that his voice can never be fully extinguished. There remains in his written and spoken words a keen insight into the universal human condition, and the universal quest for the Divine in the ordinary.

Although we've titled this collection *From the Angel's Blackboard* (reminiscent of Sheen's successful television program from decades past), the contents embrace much more than material from his subsequent series, *Life Is Worth Living*. Space limitations prohibit inclusion of all texts that are of continued interest to today's spiritual seekers; and final selections, admittedly, represent personal preference. But it is our hope that these words will touch a new generation of readers as well as those for whom Fulton J. Sheen was a source of light, hope, faith, and understanding amid the inescapable doubts and struggles and frustrations of everyday life.

The selections that follow have in many cases been abridged and edited with a contemporary sensibility in mind. To the extent possible (and comfortable), attention has been given to inclusive language. In these instances, we trust in Fulton Sheen's blessing from above. But where text did not yield easily to change, we have chosen to leave Sheen's words intact (begging in these instances for the reader's understanding). We hope that readers will bring to these selections a ready and open spirit, a simple trust, and a heart that wills to be enlarged. If but a single soul can be transformed for the better; a single mind opened to new possibilities; a single heart stirred to greater good, this volume will have served its purpose well.

A special note of thanks to the good and wonderful people at the Society for the Propagation of the Faith — in particular Bishop William J. McCormack, National Director, and James R. Borut and Florence Lee, for their generous support of this undertaking. Their help and encouragement, and especially their faith in me, are deeply appreciated. Any shortcomings are mine alone.

God Love You!

PATRICIA A. KOSSMANN
Literary Representative
The Estate of Fulton J. Sheen

Sanctifying the Moment

MILLIONS OF MEN AND WOMEN TODAY lead what has been called "lives of quiet desperation." They are panicky, worried, neurotic, fearful, and, above all, frustrated souls. And frustration results from failure — either a failure that has already occurred or a failure in prospect. Some people may become frustrated by comparing the immensity of the problems facing them with the feebleness of their resources for solving them; in such cases, they are too discouraged, too apprehensive of failure, even to try for a solution. Or they may become frustrated from a lack of someone to love, someone who will love them sufficiently in return.

The first type of frustration puts a soul in the harried position of a householder who becomes more and more depressed as the bills mount up, and money fails to materialize. He or she dreads a future reckoning. The second kind of frustration involves the feeling that life is passing quickly and that the chances for emotional fulfillment are growing less with every year. Both forms of misery are connected, then, with an unhappy individual's consciousness of the passage of time. The frustrated soul is the one most apt to shiver when seeing the old sundial warning: "It is later than you think."

All our anxieties relate to time. A human being is the only time-conscious creature. Humans alone can bring the past to mind, so that it weighs on the present moment with its accumulated heritage; and they can also bring the future into the present, so as to imagine its oc-

3

currences as happening now. No animal ever says: "I have suffered this pain for six years, and it will last until I die." But because a human being can unite the past to the present by memory, and the future to the present by imagination, it is often necessary to distract him in his sufferings — to break up the continuity of misery. All unhappiness (when there is no immediate cause for sorrow) comes from excessive concentration on the past or from extreme preoccupation with the future. The major problems of psychiatry revolve around an analysis of the despair, pessimism, melancholy, and complexes that are the inheritances of what has been or with the fears, anxieties, worries, that are the imaginings of what will be.

In addition to cases of true insanity and mental aberration — when scientific psychiatry is essential — there are many others for whom this unhappy preoccupation with the past and future has a moral basis. A conscience burdened with the guilt of past sins is fearful of divine judgment. But God in His mercy has given us two remedies for such an unhappiness. One is the Sacrament of Penance, which blots out the past by remission of our sins and lightens the future by our hope for divine mercy through continued repentance and amendment of our lives. Nothing in human experience is as efficacious in curing the memory and imagination as confession; it cleanses us of guilt, and if we follow the admonitions of Our Lord, we shall put completely out of mind our confessed sins: "No one who puts a hand to the plow and looks back is fit for the kingdom of God" (Lk 9:62). Confession also heals the imagination, eliminating its anxiety for the future; for now, with Paul, the soul cries out: "I can do all things through him who strengthens me" (Phil 4:13).

The second remedy for the ills that come to us from thinking about time is what might be called the sanctification of the moment — or the Now. Our Lord laid down the rule for us in these words: "So do not worry about tomorrow, for tomorrow will bring worries of its own. Today's trouble is enough for today" (Mt 6:34). This means that each day has its own trials; we are not to borrow troubles from tomorrow, because that day too will have its cross. We are to leave the past to divine mercy and to trust the future, whatever its trials, to God's loving providence. Each minute of life has its peculiar duty — regardless of the appearance that minute may take. The Now-moment is the moment of salvation. Each complaint against it is a defeat; each act of resignation to it is a victory.

*   *   *

The present moment includes some things over which we have control, but it also carries with it difficulties we cannot avoid — such things as a business failure, a bad cold, rain on picnic days, an unwelcome visitor, a fallen cake, a buzzer that doesn't work, a fly in the milk, and a boil on the nose the night of the dance. We do not always know why such things as sickness and setbacks happen to us, for our minds are far too puny to grasp God's plan. A person is a little like a mouse in a piano, which cannot understand why it must be disturbed by someone playing Chopin and forcing it to move off the piano wires.

When Job suffered, he posed questions to God: Why was he born, and why was he suffering? God appeared to him, but instead of answering Job's questions, He began to ask Job to answer some of the larger questions about the universe. When the Creator had finished pouring queries into the head of the creature, Job realized that the questions of God were wiser than the answers of men. Because God's ways are not our ways — because the salvation of a soul is more important than all material values — because divine wisdom can draw good out of evil — the human mind must develop acceptance of the Now, no matter how hard it may be for us to understand its freight of pain. We do not walk out of a theater because the hero is shot in the first act; we give the dramatist credit for having a plot in mind. So the soul does not walk out on the first act of God's drama of salvation — it is the last act that is to crown the play. The things that happen to us are not always susceptible to our minds' comprehension or wills' conquering; but they are always within the capacity of our faith to accept and of our wills' submission.

One question is never asked by Love, and that is "Why?" That word is used only by the three d's of doubt, deceit, and the devil. The happiness of the garden of paradise, founded on trusting love, cracked under the satanic query: "Why has God commanded you?" To true love, each wish of the beloved is a dread command — the lover even wishes that the requests were multiplied, that there might be more frequent opportunities of service. Those who love God do not protest, whatever He may ask of them, nor doubt His kindness when He sends them difficult hours. A sick person takes medicine without asking the physician to justify its bitter taste, because the patient trusts the doctor's knowledge; so the soul that has sufficient faith accepts all the events of life as gifts from God, in the serene assurance that God knows best.

Every moment brings us more treasures than we can gather. The great value of the Now, spiritually viewed, is that it carries a message God has directed personally to us. Books, sermons, and broadcasts on a religious theme have the appearance of being circular letters, meant for everyone. Sometimes, when such general appeals do appear to have a personal application, the soul gets angry and writes vicious letters to allay its uneasy conscience. Excuses can always be found for ignoring the divine law. But though moral and spiritual appeals carry God's identical message to all who listen, this is not true of the Now-moment; no one else but I am in exactly these circumstances; no one else has to carry the same burden, whether it be sickness, the death of a loved one, or some other adversity. Nothing is more individually tailored to our spiritual needs than the Now-moment; for that reason it is an occasion of knowledge that can come to no one else. This moment is my school, my textbook, my lesson. Not even Our Lord disdained to learn from His specific Now; being God, He knew all, but there was still one kind of knowledge He could experience as a human. St. Paul describes it: "Although he was a Son, he learned obedience through what he suffered" (Heb 5:8).

The University of the Moment has been built uniquely for each of us, and in comparison with the revelation God gives each in it, all other methods of learning are shallow and slow. This wisdom is distilled from intimate experience, is never forgotten; it becomes part of our character, our merit, our eternity. Those who sanctify the moment, and offer it up in union with God's will, never become frustrated — never grumble or complain. They overcome all obstacles by making them occasions of prayer and channels of merit. What were constrictions are thus made opportunities for growth. It is the modern pagan who is the victim of circumstance, and not its master. Such an individual, having no practical knowledge of God, no trust in His providence, no assurance of His love, lacks the shock absorber of faith and hope and love when difficult days come. Such a person's mind is caught within the pincers of a past he regrets or resents and a future he is afraid he cannot control. Being thus squeezed, his nature is in pain.

Those who accept God's will in all things escape such frustration by piercing the disguise of outward events to penetrate to their real character as messengers of the God they love. It is strange how differently we accept a misfortune — or even an insult — when we know who gave it to us. A teen might normally resent it very much if a well-dressed young woman accidentally stepped on her toes in a bus; but if that same teen recognized that the one who hurt her was her favorite movie star, she would probably boast of it to her friends. Demands that might seem outrageous from an acquaintance are met with happy compliance if it is a friend who asks our help. In like manner, we are able to adapt with a good grace to the demands of every Now when we recognize God's will and purpose behind the illness and the shocks and disappointments of life.

The swaddling clothes of an infant hid the Son of God in Bethlehem, and the appearance of bread and wine hides the Reality of Christ dying again on Calvary, in the Mass. This concealment of Himself that God effects with us is operative in His use of the Now to hide His will beneath the aspect of very simple, everyday things. We live our lives in dependence on such casual, common benefits as air and water; so Our Lord is pleased to receive from us in return the thousands of unimportant actions and the trifling details that make up our lives — provided that we see, even in our sorrows, "the shade of His hand outstretched caressingly." Here is the whole secret of sanctity; the method is available to everyone and deserves particular notice from those who ask:

"What can I do?" For many good souls are hungry to do great things for God. They complain that they have no opportunities for heroic virtue, no chance at the apostolate. They would be martyrs; but when a meal is late, or a bus is crowded, when the theater is filled, or the dance post-poned, or the bacon overdone, they are upset for a whole day. They miss their opportunities for loving God in the little things He asks of them. Our Lord said: "Whoever is faithful in a very little is faithful also in much" (Lk 16:10).

The Divine Beloved speaks to the soul in a whisper, but because the soul is waiting for a trumpet, it loses His command. All of us would like to make our own crosses — tailor-made trials. But not many of us wel-come the crosses God sends. Yet it is in doing perfectly the little chores He gives that saints find holiness. The big, world-shattering things many of us imagine we would like to do for God might, in the end, feed only our egotism. On the other hand, to accept the crosses of our state of life because they come from an all-loving God is to have taken the most important step in the reformation of the world, namely, the reformation of the *self*. Sanctity can be built out of patient endurance of the incessant grumbling of a spouse, the boss's habit of smoking a pipe at the office, the noise the children make with their soup, the un-expected illness, the failure to find a marital partner, the inability to get rich. All these can become occasions of merit and be made into prayers if they are borne patiently for love of One Who bears so patiently with us, despite our shortcomings, our failures, and our sins.

It is not hard to put up with others' foibles when one realizes how much God has to put up with from us. There is a legend that one day Abraham was visited in the desert by an Arab, who set up loud com-plaints of the food, the lodging, the bed, and the wine that his generous host had offered him. Finally, Abraham became exasperated and was about to put him out. God appeared to Abraham at that moment and said: "Abraham, I have stood this man for forty years; can't you put up with him for one day?"

To accept the duty of this moment for God is to touch Eternity, to escape from time. This habit of embracing the Now and glorifying

God through its demands is an act of the loving will. We do not need an intellectual knowledge of God's plan in order to accept it. When St. Paul was converted he asked merely: "Lord, what wilt Thou have me to do?" We can be warmed by a fire without knowing the chemistry of combustion, and we can be cured by a medicine without knowing its prescription. The divine will, pouring into the soul of a simple paralytic resigned to suffering, will give him a far greater understanding of theology than a professor will get from a lifetime of theoretical curiosity about religion that he does not practice. The good thief and the bad thief on the cross had the same crisis of fear and suffering — one of them complained and lost his chance for heaven that day; the other spiritualized the brief moment of suffering. Some souls win peace and sanctity from the same trials that make others rebels and nervous wrecks.

God cannot seize our wills or force us to use our trials advantageously, but neither can the devil. We are absolute dictators in deciding whether we wish to offer our will to God. And if we turn it over to God without reservation, He will do great things in us. As a chisel in the hands of Michelangelo can produce a better statue than a chisel in the hands of a child, so the human will becomes more effective when it has become a liege of God than if we try to rule alone. Our wills operating under our own power may be busy about many things, but in the end they come to nothing. Under divine power, the nothingness of our wills becomes effective, beyond our fondest dreams.

The phrase that sanctifies any moment is "Thy will be done." It was that *fiat* of our Savior in Gethsemane that initiated our redemption; it was the *fiat* of Our Lady that opened the way to the Incarnation. The word cuts all the guy ropes that attach us to the familiar, narrow things we know; it unfurls all our sails to the possibilities of the moment, and it carries one along to whatever port God wills. To say and mean "Thy will be done" is to put an end to all complaining; for whatever the moment brings to us now bears the imprint of the divine will.

There are great subjective advantages to such an act of resignation to God's will. The first is this: We escape from the power that the "accidents" of life had over us. The accidents of life are those things that interrupt our ordered existence and cancel our plans — mishaps such as a sickness that forces us to defer a trip, or the summons of the telephone when we are tuned in to our favorite television program. It is a medical fact that tense and worried people have more accidents resulting in fractures than those who have a clear conscience and a divine goal in life. Some men and women complain that they "never get a break," that the world is their enemy, that they have "bad luck." Persons resigned to God's holy will utter no such complaint; whatever comes along, they welcome it. The disorganized, self-centered soul tries to impose his or her own will on the universe — and always fails. Such a one is in constant pain for the same reason that a stomach is in pain if it tries a diet of ground glass — it is living in contrast to the divine purpose. Such a soul cannot see how the thing bothering him at this moment can be justified, for he judges all that occurs by the narrow, unrealistic standard: "Is this what I had planned?" But life is a larger business than the egotist assumes. It will not be reduced to so small a thing that it can fit into any human brain. A human cannot even devise a "system" at roulette that will provide for all the possible contingencies of one small, spinning wheel. How can he possibly have the *hubris* to expect the immensely various world about him — its human beings with their own souls, its willful changes of climate, its complex possibilities of every sort — to accommodate itself to his infinitesimal capacity for making plans?

The difference between people who never get the breaks and those who make every Now an occasion for thanking God is this: The latter live in an area of love greater than their desire to "have their way." As a waif on the streets suffers misfortunes that the child in a loving family does not know, so the person who has not learned to place full trust in God suffers reverses and disasters that would not appear as troubles to loving souls. God does not show Himself equally to all creatures. He does show us how to turn everything to joy. This does not mean God is unfair, but only that it is impossible for even Him to show Himself to certain hearts under some conditions. The sunlight has no favorites, but it cannot shine as well on a dusty mirror as on a polished one.

In the order of divinity, there is nothing accidental; there is never a collision of blind forces, hurting us, at random. There is, instead, the meeting of a divine will and a human will that has a perfect trust that ultimate good is meant for it, although it may not understand *how* until eternity. Every human being is, in point of fact, like a baby in the arms of its loving mother, who sometimes administers medicine. God sends us all the happenings of everyday life as so many invitations to self-perfection in His service. The baby cries, the egotist protests, but the saint in the arms of God is content, because she knows God knows exactly what is best for her. Thus the bitter and the sweet, the joys and sorrows of each moment, are viewed as the raw material of sanctity. "We know that all things work together for good for those who love God, who are called according to his purpose" (Rom 8:28).

Every commonplace event now becomes a mystery, because it is the bearer of the divine will. Nothing is insignificant or dull — everything can be sanctified, just as goats and sheep, fish and wheat, grapes and eyes of needles were given dignity as parables of the Kingdom of God. Things the worldly-wise would trample under foot become as precious to saints as pearls, for they see "sermons in stones and good in everything." Even the bitterest of life's punishments are known to be joys in the making, rare spiritual treasures underneath their harsh and ugly appearances.

... It will seem strange to the worldling, but even our enemies — even those who cheat or malign us — can become occasions for advancement toward union with God. All contradictions can be turned to good by those who have put their trust in God. Seeing the trial as issuing from the divine hand, one never has to wonder how to meet it, nor question why it came, nor seek defense against it. Each trial is an occasion for faith and an opportunity for virtue. Having put oneself in the deeper dimension of divine love, one knows, as a child in a loving family knows, that even what is not understood is done kindly and for the best. There finally comes a period of union with God when everything seems unreal except divine love. The soul in the midst of trials and aches becomes like an airplane flying — it follows the beam of God's will through the fog and mist.

It is for each of us to decide what we are working for — what reward we wish for. For everyone is trying for some prize. If we are not interested in eternal merit, in gaining ultimate union with God, then we are interested in winning the applause of others, or the approbation of a single person, at the very least. Our Divine Lord knew that most souls were interested only in temporal applause when He said: "Beware of practicing your piety before others in order to be seen by them; for then you have no reward from your Father in heaven" (Mt 6:1). If we do good deeds to others because we love them on the human level, we receive a human recompense in their affection — but not a divine supernatural recompense.

"If you love those who love you, what credit is that to you? For even sinners love those who love them. If you lend to those from whom you hope to receive, what credit is that to you? Even sinners lend to sinners, to receive as much again. But love your enemies, do good, and lend, expecting nothing in return. Your reward will be great, and you will be children of the Most High; for he is kind to the ungrateful and the wicked" (Lk 6:32–35).

Our Lord lists trivial little acts of goodness — such as giving a drink of cold water to a stranger — and assures us that a supernatural reward awaits us if we do them *for His sake,* for love of Him. But if we wish to seek these supernatural prizes, we will have to satisfy certain conditions. These are not unlike the conditions set down for gaining competence on the natural plane. Suppose someone has the ideal of being a good runner. Three conditions are essential: (1) He or she must be a born runner. There are certain capacities and talents, certain structures of bones and muscles, certain powers of breathing, that are never acquired. They are given. They constitute the capacity to run. Track scouts can look at school children before they have received any training and can tell whether they will ever be runners. (2) The individuals must be free to decide for themselves. There are some who have a talent for running but who refuse to go out for the team. If someone competes only because forced to, the chances are that that person will never do it well. (3) Given the talent for running, and the desire for it, the actions a runner performs must all bear on his or her goal. Excessive smoking or drinking, laziness, or disregard for the proper technique could ruin every realization of the runner's talent. All a runner does must be directed toward the goal of championship.

Apply this to the soul who wishes to run in the race of eternal salvation, to win the incorruptible crown. Three conditions are again required: (1) A person must be born to the supernatural order by baptism; he or she must enter into the state of grace, which gives a person the capacity, the gift, the talent, for the supernatural. To gain a human reward, we operate on the human level; to gain a reward from God, we must become children of God — the branches must be united to the Vine. All the good acts of a person in the state of grace merit salvation through God's mercy — for God is the principal cause of merit. "Only by God's grace I am what I am, and the grace He has shown me has not been without fruit; I have worked harder than all of them, or rather, it was not I, but the grace of God working with me" (1 Cor 15:10). (2) The soul must be free. There is no merit in virtue if one is forced to practice it or it is followed through necessity. When our human wills respond to the divine action, they are only secondary to God's grace as a cause of merit — but although secondary, our contribution is a very real one. God and the person cooperate. (3) Whatever the soul does ought to be a morally good act, one destined by its nature to recompense in supernatural coin. There are no indifferent acts when one is in the state of grace; an act is either meritorious or it is not.

Assume that the acts we do are morally good in themselves. Then each task or duty is like a blank check; the value it possesses depends on whose name is signed to it, on whether it is done for the I's sake or for God's sake. Motive is what makes the saint; sanctification does not depend on our geography, nor on our work or circumstances. Some people imagine that if they were in another place, or married to a different spouse, or had a different job, or had more money, they could do God's work so much better. The truth is that it makes no difference where they are; it all depends on whether what they are doing is God's will and done for love of Him.

We would all like to make our own crosses; but since Our Lord did not make His own, neither do we make ours. We can take whatever God gives us, and we can make the supernatural best of it. The typist working on routine letters, the street cleaner carrying a broom, the farmer tilling the field, the doctor bending over a patient, the lawyer trying a case, the student with books, the sick in their isolation and pain, the teacher drilling pupils, the mother dressing the children — every such task, every such duty, can be ennobled and spiritualized if it is done in God's Name.

[LIFT UP YOUR HEART]

The more conscious we are of the passing of time, the less we enjoy ourselves.

*   *   *

Temporal goods cannot be enjoyed all at once. The characteristic of the temporal enjoyment of various goods and objects is that they must be enjoyed in succession. Some begin where others leave off. When something new comes, something that we had before is taken away. We cannot have the ripe wisdom and the reflective serenity of maturity together with the impetuousness and the adventurousness of youth. All are good; yet none can be enjoyed except in the season of life appropriate to it. What is true individually is true socially. However much we may gain by what we call the advance in civilization, something has to be surrendered.

[LIFE IS WORTH LIVING]

Conscience,
the Interior Sinai

ONSCIENCE is an interior government, exercising the same functions as all human government: namely, legislative, executive, and judicial. It has its Congress, its President, and its Supreme Court: It makes its laws, it witnesses our actions in relation to the laws, and finally it judges us.

First of all, conscience legislates. One needs only to live to know that there is in each of us an interior Sinai, from which is promulgated, amid the thunder and lightning of daily life, a law telling us to do good and avoid evil. That interior voice fills us with a sense of responsibility, reminding us, not that we *must* do certain things, but that we *ought* to do certain things, for the difference between a machine and a person is the difference between *must* and *ought*. Without even being consulted, conscience plays its legislative role, pronouncing some actions to be in themselves evil and unjust, and others in themselves moral and good. Hence, when citizens fail to see a relationship existing between a human law and the law of their own conscience, they feel that they are free to disobey, and their justifying cry is, "My conscience tells me it is wrong."

Second, conscience not only is legislative, in the sense that it lays down a law, but it is also executive, in the sense that it witnesses the application of the law to actions. An imperfect but helpful analogy is to be found in our own government. Congress passes a law, then the president witnesses and approves it, thus applying the law to the lives of citizens. In like manner, conscience executes laws in the sense that it witnesses the fidelity of our actions to the law. Aided by memory, it tells us the value of our actions; tells us if we were total masters of ourselves; the extent to which passion, environment, force, and fury influence us; whether our consequences were foreseen or unforeseen; shows us, as in a mirror, the footsteps of all our actions; points its finger at the vestiges of our decisions; comes to us as a true witness and says: "I was there; I saw you do it. You had such and such an intention." In the administration of human justice the law can call together only those witnesses who have known me externally, but conscience as a witness summons not only those who saw me, but summons also *me who know myself*. And whether I like it or not, I cannot lie to what it witnesses against me.

Finally, conscience not only lays down laws, not only witnesses my obedience or disobedience to them, but it also judges me accordingly. The breast of every person bears a silent court of justice. Conscience is the judge, sitting in judgment, handing down decisions with such authority as to admit of no appeal, for no one can appeal a judgment that one brings against oneself. That is why there gather about the bar of conscience all the feelings and emotions associated with right and wrong — joy and sorrow, peace and remorse, self-approval and fear, praise and blame.

If I do wrong, it fills me with a sense of guilt from which there is no escape, for if the inmost sanctuary of my being is assaulted by the stern voice of this judge, I am driven out of myself by myself. Whence, then, can I fly but to myself with the sickening sense of guilt, remorse, and disgrace, which is the very hell of the soul? If, on the contrary, conscience approves my action, then there settles upon me, like the quiet of an evening dew, the joy that is a stranger to the passing pleasures of sense. The world may call me guilty, its courts may judge me criminal, its irons may weight down my flesh and bones like deep-sea anchors, but my soul builds a paradise within, against the raging opposition without, and floods it with an interior peace that the world cannot give and that the insults of the world cannot take from me.

[THE MORAL UNIVERSE]

There are many people who go about their duties in the daytime with an apparent peace of mind but who at night, because of an unrequited sense of guilt, feel those pangs that make them afraid of the dark. As a person may have a clear head and an active mind but also may have a disease of the brain that will later reveal itself, so many a person may be apparently upright and noble-minded, generous and tolerant, yet be gradually eaten away from the inside by a hidden guilt. That is why the spiritual ancients of old cried out, "Cleanse me from my secret faults, O Lord."

How can we avoid these modern sufferings that stem from secret guilt? Many of them would yield to nightly examination of conscience.

[PEACE OF SOUL]

Great Moments
of Decision

N APOLEON HELD THAT THE FATE of every battle was decided in the space of about five minutes. All the maneuvering and all the preparations led up to the strategic moment of crisis. If the leader had vision to take advantage of those few moments, the enemy's rout would be complete; if, however, the leader allowed it to pass, defeat was certain. In one battle his forces were halted before a bridge over a deep ravine. If the bridge was not crossed, the battle would be lost. The soldiers were afraid to advance upon it inasmuch as it was swept by the fire of Austrian cannons. Napoleon snatched the flag from the standard bearer and rushed onto the bridge shouting, "Forward to save your general!" The effect upon the soldiers was electric, and in that five minutes the battle was decided.

It could very well be that the life of every person is not so much decided by the routine events of every day, but rather during two or three great moments of decision that happen in every life. As Shakespeare put it:

> There is a tide in the affairs of men
> Which taken at the flood, leads on to fortune;
> Omitted, all the voyage of their life
> Is bound in shallows and in miseries.

If the opportunity is allowed to slip by unimproved, success turns into failure. There is the name of a place that signifies such a turning point in human lives and that is Kadesh-Barnea, which is situated on the southern border of the Promised Land. There came a point in the pilgrimage when the children of Israel were within striking distance of their inheritance. They sent out spies, twelve of them, to report on the land they were about to take. The majority report, made by the representatives of ten of the tribes, was that the land could not be taken because the cities were too fortified and the enemy too numerous. The minority report, brought in by Joshua and Caleb, was turned down despite the fact that God had told the people through Moses that they would possess the land. It was this point in the journey, like the five minutes in Napoleon's battle, that determined their future. With the fruit of their tribulations within their grasp they refused to take it and thus had to continue wandering in the desert for many years.

There is a Kadesh-Barnea in every nation, a critical moment when it has the power to turn back a force from without, or a corrosion from within. It has been called "a time of visitation" when power is given to vanquish, but if not seized, turns the nation into a kind of cadaver on which the scavengers feed.

There is also a Kadesh-Barnea in every person's spiritual life. One's background may be filled with unbelief, guilt, dishonesties, adulteries, and any of the seven pallbearers of the soul. Then there comes a moment of illumination to the mind, perhaps in a moment of sickness or a startling thought while reading, or the vision of innocence in a child. If this grace is responded to, a person is lifted out of himself, cuts connections with the past and starts out on a new career and new paths, with heaven shining in his face.

People too often play with opportunity as a toy, and when their eyes are opened to see its value, lo! it has vanished. Many reach the margin of a glorious destiny and then turn back to the desert. The path of duty, in a flash of the eye, becomes very plain, but self-indulgence makes the soul as blind as a mole. Were we to deal honestly with these pious inclinations and whisperings of conscience, we should see through the thin guise of our own pretenses and then strip the veneer of insincerity from our deeds. There is often a conspiracy in everyone against self; we hunt for excuses to cover up disobedience, but in a single moment, life can be changed — not by pulling oneself through the power of one's own will, but by a response to heaven's inspirations that leaves the deserts of the world behind.

[GUIDE TO CONTENTMENT]

It is not true that acknowledging our sins as sins induces a guilt complex or morbidity. Because children go to school, do they develop an ignorance complex? Because the sick go to the doctor, do they have a sickness complex? The students concentrate, not upon their own ignorance, but upon the wisdom of the teacher; the sick concentrate, not upon their illness, but upon the curative powers of the doctor; and sinners, seeing their sins for what they are, concentrate, not on their own guilt, but upon the recuperative powers of the Divine Physician.

There is *no evidence whatever* to sustain the position of some modern psychiatrists that consciousness of sin tends to make a person morbid. To call someone an escapist because he or she asks God for forgiveness is like calling a householder whose home is on fire an escapist because he sends for the fire department. If there is anything morbid in the sinner's responsible admission of a violated relationship with divine love, this is a jovial sanity compared with the real and terrible morbidity that comes to those who are sick and who refuse to admit their illness.

[PEACE OF SOUL]

Encounter with God

PEOPLE TODAY do not come to God through the order of the universe; they come to God through disorder within their own selves. The argument is still valid that the heavens do declare the glory of God, but we rarely see the stars, and neon lights hardly reflect anything. When men could see nature, they argued back to nature's God. In the complexity of modern civilization, however, we see ourselves less as living in nature, but more as living within ourselves.

It must not be assumed that it is only through the order and finality of the universe that one comes to the Creator; one can also come to the knowledge of the light through shadows. Health is more often appreciated after a sickness. The modern world has many encounters with God, but it does not know that it has met God. Our encounters with God may come in a moment of disgust or sickness, after some kind of excess, or in a holy desire to be like another person who spends himself and is spent on his neighbor; or it may be through a pious inspiration.

These encounters or soul skirmishes do not necessarily mean that one begins to know God. Jacob wrestled all the night without knowing who his opponent was until the break of day. The young man who was born blind was questioned by the Pharisees as to who it was who cured him. He answered, "Whether He is a sinner I do not know. One thing I do know, that whereas I was blind, now I see" (Jn 9:25).

The woman at the well who was living in adultery did not know immediately Who it was Who confronted her at midday at the well. She first thought Him to be a Jew, then a gentleman, then a prophet, then a messiah, but only at the end did she recognize Him to be the Savior of the World.

One of the most common encounters is in the moment of emptiness, boredom, or fed-up-ness. This comes generally after a sensible pleasure or a mood of exaltation, as when the honeymoon is over and the bills come into the kitchen. It is an hour of need, and every need cries out for fulfillment. The need may be compared to a hollow space that rattles as it cries out to be filled; every void is related to a desire, a groping, a reaching out, a yearning for something.

This need can be multiplied, such as with food for the stomach, learning for the mind, companionship for the heart. But whatever it be, it has one basic characteristic: *The longing cannot be stilled by our own power, but with the aid of another.* There is need of some extraneous agent to fill up the cavity. The individual alone feels impotent and powerless. Associated with this need is what a distinguished Viennese psychiatrist, Dr. Igor Caruso, has called "the need of salvation." The One Who can enter is God, but there is no one who can force Him to enter. The human being can bar the doors to the divine visitor.

It is here that one comes face to face with the problem of existence. The well-known Jewish psychiatrist Dr. Viktor Frankl, who passed through two concentration camps, one Nazi, the other Communist, had ample evidence to study the findings of meaning and purpose, even in trial. Some turned a deaf ear to the encounter with God, and of them he writes, "Often, existential frustration leads to sexual compensation. The sexual libido often becomes most rampant in an existential vacuum." Others, he said, became religious through this encounter, and he defines a religious person as "one who actually does not feel responsible to something, but to someone." From that point on, one learns he can endure any "how?" in the world, because he knows the "why?" — namely, that all things compensate unto good to those who are called to fulfill their need of salvation.

Religion Has Moved
to the Subconscious

W E LIVE in what might be called the Age of Bad Conscience. We cover it up by denying responsibility; we find
scapegoats; we attack religion and all who have to do
with conscience as if their extinction might give us immunity from that
distinction between right and wrong. If any science is unpopular today
it is certainly theology, particularly when couched in the language of
reason and concepts that are alien to our moods and frustrations. But
this does not mean there is no religion in modern man. There is; but it
has moved from the area of conscience to the subconscious.

We say "religion" because nothing that is in a person escapes the
providence and mercy of God. It is just as easy for God to work in a
cellar as a first floor, as well in the realm of emotions as in the realm
of reason. The very uneasiness of the subconscious mind with its fears
and dreads and anxieties is a kind of chaos for what might be called an
anti-peace. But this chaos might be likened to the chaos in the second
verse of Genesis, when the first creative word was rejected and left
nothing behind but disorder. And over that chaos the Spirit hovered
like a dove bringing order out of the disorder of creation, as the Holy
Spirit, later on, breathing over Mary, brought order out of the chaos
of humanity.

God probably speaks more frequently through our subconscious mind than through our conscious mind, simply because our self-consciousness puts up obstacles to Him. God can guide us quite naturally in a particular direction without our being aware of it. What was it, for example, that induced Paul Claudel, an agnostic and un-believer, to enter Notre Dame Cathedral at midnight on Christmas, and ultimately to receive the gift of faith? Here was a reasonable man who was guided unreasonably. Very often stupid people come to God through very reasonable arguments, and reasonable people come to God through no argument at all.

There is an outward force operating on the subconscious mind that changes its direction. If a ball is thrown across a room, it will go in an unhindered path unless a foot or a hand is put out to divert it. The subconscious mind may be governed once by vice, and then suddenly turn in the direction of love. This change of attitude and transforma-tion requires that an outside power or Spirit that acts like a catalyst bring together discordant elements into a new unity.

If a person corresponds with this impulse from without, it is like turning on radio waves of speech, music, humor, and learning that fill the air. But these blessings do not affect the person until he or she is at the proper wavelength and tunes in.

Sometimes our dreams reveal the religious and moral state of the subconscious mind. Carl Jung holds that every dream is a manifesta-tion of our spiritual state; the interpretation, however, is not always easy. E. N. Ducker tells the story of a woman who came to him with a dream that an old china closet was given to her that she did not want. She took it to a dealer, convinced that it was worthless, and he paid her ten thousand dollars. He took a piece of sandpaper and rubbed off the gaudy paint, and there underneath it was gold. After she got the money, she tried to find the person who gave it to her, but he was gone. Ducker explained the dream as follows: The china closet was herself, whom she regarded as worthless, in monetary value worth only a few cents. The dealer was identified as Our Lord, Who saw her real worth, that is, in terms of gold, a genuine treasure. The gaudy paint that cov-ered the gold was her conscious approach to life. She was doing things to catch the eye, to appear significant, to impress the world, and to endow herself with value. The ten thousand dollars was her true value, which the Lord put upon her. She tried to find Him again, but He was gone, with the result that she had to accept the value that the Lord had put upon her.

Jung says that very often dreams are also compensations for wrong opinions we have of ourselves. He tells of one of his patients who had an exalted opinion of himself and was unaware that everyone who knew him was irritated by his air of superiority. He came to Dr. Jung with a dream in which he had seen a drunken tramp rolling into a ditch — a sight that provoked him to say, "It is terrible to see how low a man can fall." The psychiatrist says that it was evidently a dream in part compensating for his own inflated opinion of himself; but there was something more to it than that. It turned out that he had a brother who was a degenerate alcoholic. What the dream also revealed was that his superior attitude was compensating the brother.

The world is not as irreligious as it seems at first glance. Religion has moved out of churches, to a large extent, to cope with our frustrations, despairs, shames, and neuroses. The only mistake the churches can make in the new order is to assume that everybody must come to them instead of their going to everybody.

[GUIDE TO CONTENTMENT]

Health
and Holiness

THE ACCUMULATED WISDOM of the human race has always acknowledged that there was some kind of relationship between peace of soul and health. "A healthy mind in a healthy body" is only an abbreviation of a statement from the Latin poet Juvenal, who wrote in his satires, "Your prayer must be that you may have a sound mind in a sound body." A more modern poet, Francis Thompson, wrote, "Holiness is an oil which increases a hundredfold the energies of the body, which is the wick." The Austrians had a proverb: "A sad saint is a sorry sort of a saint."

Today, however, medicine and psychiatry are combining to prove that there is some intrinsic relationship between holiness and health. The French tradition of medicine has always believed in a long interrogation of the patient in order to view the drama of his human life. Recently there has been published a treatise by the well-known Swiss psychiatrist Dr. Paul Tournier, entitled *The Healing of Persons*, which is a contribution to a synthesis of modern psychology and the Christian faith. He holds that the physical problems of a person's life often correspond to mental problems and both of these, in turn, to spiritual problems. There is no physical reform possible without a moral reform. And there is no moral reform without a spiritual renewal. This boils down to saying that behavior and a mode of life are very important actors in determining health. Symptoms, he holds, may be exaggerated forms of normal defense reactions; they are abnormal as far as disease is concerned, but they may be normal as far as the defensive reaction is concerned.

A confirmation of this idea comes from Dr. Swain of Boston, who wrote of 270 cases in which the patient was cured on being freed from fear, worry, and resentment. His conclusion was that 60 percent of arthritis cases had their origin in moral conflict. Everyone is familiar with the conclusions of Dr. K. A. Menninger, who stresses the influence of the state of mind on the condition of those suffering from high blood pressure. The latter often seems to be a sort of physical expression of a moral hypertension that paralyzes it. Dr. Alexis Carel, speaking of the alarming increase of neurosis and psychosis over the last hundred years, states that this increase "can be more dangerous for civilization than infectious diseases. Mental diseases by themselves are more numerous than all other diseases put together." Dr. Tournier holds that "all functional disturbances and, *a fortiori*, all neuroses, may be seen to involve thus a secret flight into disease. This, of course, is not to say that the disease itself is imaginary.... How many women there are who have a migraine every time they receive an invitation to visit their hostile in-laws."

Some years ago, Dr. C. G. Jung made a statement that has been quoted many times: "During the past thirty years, people from all civilized countries of the earth have consulted me.... Among all my patients in the second half of life — that is to say, over thirty-five — there has not been one whose problem in the last resort was not that of finding a religious outlook on life. It is safe to say that every one of them fell ill because he had lost that which the living religions of every age have given to their followers, and none of them had really been healed who did not regain his religious outlook."

The vocation of a doctor should not be underrated. The doctor's ideal is not just to cure a patient of neuralgia or phobias, but also to be at one and the same time an educator, a politician, a representative of

God, a philosopher, and a theologian, not in the sense of taking over completely any of these functions, but rather in recognizing that every sick person in the world has, to some extent, a combination of three disorders: physical, psychic, and spiritual.

[GUIDE TO CONTENTMENT]

A complex according to the usage of contemporary psychology is a group of memories and desires of which we are not conscious but that nevertheless affect our personality. An anxiety complex would be a system of unhappy memories submerged in the unconscious and producing many kinds of symptoms. Everyone has anxiety; fortunately, everyone does not have an anxiety complex.

The difference between peace of soul and discontent comes from the *kind* of anxiety we have; the broadest division of all is between anxiety over the things of time and the values of eternity. Of the first, Our Lord said, "Be not anxious, for your Heavenly Father knows you have need of these things" (Mt 6:8). The second kind of anxiety is normal because it is bound up with human freedom and is a result of our creatureliness. This anxiety is a restlessness with anything short of the perfect happiness which is God. . . .

[PEACE OF SOUL]

God Is Immanent
in the World
by His Wisdom

ALL THINGS in the world of art must have been made according to a plan. There never was a chisel touched to marble, or a brush to canvas, or a dome thrown against the vault of heaven's blue, but that some idea preceded it. In a perfect manner, everything in this world has been made according to certain ideas existing in the mind of God from all eternity. God, being Perfect Intelligence, must be, therefore, possessed of the models, ideas, or representations of all the things He wishes to call into the light of day. Every tree, every flower, every bird, every thing, has had its spiritual model in the divine mind. And just as the ideas of a sculptor are imitable *ad extra*, so too the ideas of all things that God possesses are likewise imitable *ad extra*. These ideas, which from our point of view are multiple but really are one in the divine mind and identical with His Being, are called Archetypal Ideas, and in relation to immanence three conclusions may be drawn.

God is present in the universe in somewhat the same manner as an artist is present in his work of art. Just as the idea the painter has of the Blessed Mother is present on his canvas, so too the ideas God

has of things are present in things as exemplars. These divine Archetypal Ideas reflected in things, as the very rational plan of their being,
are called forms, as in the mind they are called ideas (and sometimes
forms). Everything in the world has its form, which is the reason for
its intelligibility, and makes it what it is. A tree is a tree in virtue of
its form (not external shape, but internal participation or reflection of
the Archetypal Ideas) and for that reason differs from a camel, which
has a different form. A hint of this philosophy is given in the familiar
lines of Joyce Kilmer:

> Poems are made by fools like me,
> But only God can make a tree.

Not only is God present in things as the wisdom that planned them,
but in the richness and variety of His wisdom. Being infinite, His wisdom reaches to the abyss of all things that are known and can be
known. Quite naturally, no created thing could perfectly express the
depth and variety of His knowledge; only an uncreated and single
Word can express it, and that is the Logos or the Son. It was fitting
that God became present by His wisdom, not only in one thing, but in
many. What one created thing failed to reveal, the other might dis-
close. Thus creation became like a great orchestra, with thousands
of instruments blending their various notes, and yet all cooperating
to produce the beautiful harmony in which heaven and earth declare
forth the wisdom of their omnipotent Creator.

Finally, God's wisdom participating in things is not only the reason
for their being and their richness, but it also explains our own intelligibility. Why, in the ultimate analysis, do we know? We know, not
because we invent, but because we discover — discover the wisdom
of God hidden in the things that He has made. Every material thing
in the universe is made up of matter and form. Matter makes it individual; the form, which is the architect within, is the reflection of the
divine idea. God, as it were, wrapped up His ideas in matter, just as He
has wrapped up the soul in a body.

But knowledge is impossible so long as the form or idea or the reason of intelligibility is hidden by matter. Knowledge is spiritual. If the human mind is ever to know things rationally, it must have a power above that of the animals, a capacity for stripping off the matter from the idea, or else penetrating through the matter with a vision akin to the X ray. This power Almighty God has given to the human mind in what has been called the "active intellect," which has the power, once it enters into sensible contact with things, to grasp their essence, or the form that makes them what they are. But since the form is the participation of the Archetypal Idea of that thing in the divine mind — as the cathedral is the participation of the idea in the mind of the architect — it follows that in knowing the essence or nature of things, the mind knows the likeness of the divine ideas existing in things. Thus, in an indirect way, the wisdom of God becomes immanent in our own minds through the intermediary of things. This is the fundamental reason why things are true. Truth is a conformity between the mind and things: *adaequatio rei et intellectus*. My idea of a tree is true if it conforms to the material thing before me that my senses represent to be a tree. Everything in this world is true inasmuch as it corresponds with the idea that God had in mind in making it. In this sense there is absolute truth. St. Thomas Aquinas says:

> God's own being is not only conformed to His intellect, but His act of understanding is the measure and cause of every other being and of every other intellect, and He is Himself His own existence and act of understanding. Whence it follows not only that Truth is in Him, but He is Truth itself, and the Sovereign and First Truth.*

If things are true because they correspond to the divine mind, likewise in a derived sense, our minds enjoy truth when they correspond to the things made according to the ideas of God immanent in them by participation, thanks to the Creative Act.

Summa Contra Gentiles, i, q. 16, a. 5.

In the divine order of things, the Immanence of God in creation by wisdom is meant to describe a circular process. God made things intelligently; we discover their intelligibility thanks to our own intellect, and make them immanent in us by an act of understanding. By lifting ourselves up to that Supreme Truth, the source of all gifts, we lift up the material world as well, and thus all things find their way back again to God.

[PHILOSOPHY OF RELIGION]

Knowledge is acquired; wisdom is infused. Knowledge comes from the outside; it is learned and absorbed. Wisdom is infused, and comes to us as an illumination.... We need wisdom to make big decisions, and the right answer comes from God Who has a destiny for us. God is longing to fulfill it in us for the benefit of ourselves and others.

[ON BEING HUMAN]

Habits

OW DO WE break bad habits and cultivate good habits? There must be a new ideal or else a revival of an ideal that has been forgotten. Without a motivation or reason, there is no impetus or challenge to change our habits. It is never enough to tell people that they must give up something, because the giving up can create an emptiness and a void. Unless the house is filled with goodness, evil will come to it. Rather, there must be an exchange of one thing for another. An exchange based upon what we are willing to surrender for another. An exchange is based upon what we are willing to surrender for another thing.

Zaccheus was a dishonest politician and income-tax collector, but once he found a new ideal through the visit of our Blessed Lord to his home, he made restitution. Mary Magdalene surrendered evil habits for virtue through the vision of divine purity. One of the aphorisms that is inclined to destroy character is the one that states, "It makes no difference what you believe, it all depends on how you act." The psychological fact is that we act upon our beliefs. If beliefs and ideals are wrong, our actions will be wrong.

At the beginning, it is extremely important to cultivate the highest ideals, that we may act upon those ideals. While Paul acted on the ideal of hate, he persecuted; when he changed his ideal, he became the great Apostle. When one has discovered a new ideal, such a one then is prepared to make sacrifices for that ideal, on the basis of exchange.

The difference between dieting and fasting is the difference in ideal. One fasts for the sake of the soul; one diets for the sake of the body. A person, for example, would be much more successful in dieting if, instead of just resolving to give up desserts, he or she said, "I will go without desserts and spend the equivalent of what I would have spent by giving it to help feed the poor of the world."

Even when we have developed and recognized a new ideal, it is still necessary to have an outside power to aid us, namely, the grace of God. "Can the Ethiopian change his skin or the leopard his spots?" A body that is set in motion will continue in the direction of the motion unless moved by a contrary force. We can become so enslaved by bad habits that it is impossible for us to break the chains.

Once we are caught in the clutches of an evil habit and travel in the direction of vice, it takes a divine power to turn us round and make us go in another direction. A folded paper cannot alter its structure. Trousers that have lost the crease cannot crease themselves. There is need of an iron outside of the trousers to restore the crease. A metal rod bent in one direction will remain bent that way always unless it is plunged into fire and heat. The body cannot always heal itself; there is need of medicine from the outside. The mind cannot educate itself without teachers, nor can evil habits be overcome except by what is called the grace of God, which is the infusion of a Power that makes us participate in the divine nature.

Once the mind has a new ideal or philosophy of life, once it has recognized that it is poor in spirit and needs an energy from outside, there must be a cooperation on its part through an act of the will. A distinction must be made between a wishing and a willing; a wish may recognize an ideal, but it makes no effort to follow it. The act of the will, however, is resolute and determined. The purpose of the will is to regulate impulses and urges, and to choose amid conflicting ideas, and to cooperate with the grace of God. "The road to hell is paved with good intentions," as the saying goes. There is no self-realizing power in mere aspiration. After each drink, Rip Van Winkle said, "I'll not count this time."

The purpose of the will is *to eradicate the desire of evil* in virtue of the ideal. The Rubicon must be crossed and all bridges burned behind.

Should the breaking off of the evil habit be gradual or immediate? The answer of Our Blessed Lord is that there should be an abrupt breaking. "If your right eye causes you to sin, tear it out and throw it away" (Mt 5:29). If there is anything that causes us to stumble, for example, neglecting study because of excessive novel reading, the remedy is an entire excision.

Excessive drinking is not to be cured by taking fewer and fewer drinks, any more than wife-beating is to be cured by limiting wife-beating to Wednesdays and Fridays. All the outward networks must be abandoned in order to keep the citadel. How changed the world would be if we worked as hard at being good as we work at making ourselves comfortable or beautiful!

The resolution must be applied to specific acts and must result in deeds rather than in a concentration on the evil habit in general. One cannot break a bundle of sticks when they are tied together; but they can be broken one by one. An action has a reflex effect on the mind. Do a kind act, and it begets a kindly attitude. Allow the mind to taste the joy of a virtuous deed, and it will call for its repetition. Very often the question is asked, "I have a bad temper; how can I get rid of it?" There is no such thing as a bad temper; the temper merely means that the individual has a large number of anger acts strung together. If the temper is to be controlled, it will do no good, for example, to grit one's teeth, stick one's hands in one's pockets, and resolve not to have a bad temper. It does no good to make a resolution to improve one's health. That resolution must be broken down into specific acts concerning health. So with any vice — progress is made not by dealing with the general features but with little jots and tittles. Once the principle of honesty is laid down, then the practice of honesty must refer to specific acts of honesty. To have a good idea and not act upon it hurts character. Rousseau inspired the mothers of France to nurse their own children and yet abandoned his own.

One must put oneself in an environment suitable for the development of a good habit. The habit of temperance cannot be developed at a bar, nor the habit of study at cocktail parties. Vigilance is necessary; so is the avoiding of "occasions of sin," namely, those persons, places, or things that facilitate reversions into the old habits. A bad atmosphere corrupts health, and evil companions corrupt morals. A change of moral climate is necessary for character regeneration. Diseases are more contagious than health; vices are more contagious than virtues. The manners of a child reflect the language the child hears at home. A healthy moral environment diminishes the possibility of a relapse; even if there be a relapse, the good environment will aid one to escape from it.

We are doing very well in education and training of the intellect, but there could be a greater increase of the training of the will and the formation of right habits or the cultivation of virtue. Character is not in the intellect; character is in the will. Our choices, decisions, or motivations make us what we are. If our decisions are wrong, our characters will be wrong, regardless of how much we know. Education is more than acquired information. Culture is more than a college education. The only way to change someone is to change his or her fundamental resolutions. No amount of information can do that effectively.

It is not enough to change certain details of our life; it is character as a whole that must be changed. As Michelangelo said, "Lord, take me away from myself and make me pleasing to Thee." If our character is not changed on the inside, but only by the externals, we become like a person cleaning windowpanes on a cold morning. As he scratches frost away on one pane, it quickly forms on another pane. Starting a fire inside the room would clean all the windows. A new love, a divine love, must be kindled within the heart — then the evil disappears. As St. Augustine said, "Love God and then do whatever you wish," because if you love God, you will never do anything to hurt Love.

[LOVE, MARRIAGE AND CHILDREN]

Life Is Worth Living?

I S LIFE WORTH LIVING, or is it dull and monotonous? Life is monotonous if it is meaningless; it is *not* monotonous if it has a purpose.

The prospect of seeing the same program on television for a number of weeks is this problem in minor form. Will not repetition of the same format, the same personality, the same chalk, the same blackboard, and the same angel create monotony? Repetition does generally beget boredom. However, two beautiful compensations have been given a television audience to avoid such boredom: One is a dial, the other is a wrist. Put both together, and all the forces of science and advertising vanish into nothingness.

Life is monotonous if it has no goal or purpose. When we do not know why we are here or where we are going, then life is full of frustrations and unhappiness. When there is no goal or overall purpose, people generally concentrate on motion. Instead of working toward an ideal, they keep changing the ideal and calling it "progress." They do not know where they are going, but they are certainly "on their way." Life is then like a radio in the early days. Remember? No one seemed to be interested in getting a particular program. They were interested only in picking up distant places, sitting up all night, turning the dial. The next morning they would say with glee, "You know, at three o'clock last night I got Washington, then Mobile, and I even heard Peoria."

Those who have no ultimate destiny for life really can never say they are making progress; if there is no fixed point, they can never say whether they are getting to their goal or not. Life under these circumstances is boring. A sculptor after hacking and cutting away at a block of marble all day was asked, "What are you making?" He said, "I really don't know. I haven't seen the plans."

People live ten, twenty, thirty, even fifty years without a plan. No wonder they find their existence humdrum and tiresome. If they were farmers, they would probably plant wheat one week, root it up and plant barley the next; then dig up the barley and plant watermelon; then dig up the watermelon another week and plant oats. Fall comes around, and they have no harvest; if they repeated that process for years, they could go crazy. It is the meaninglessness of life that makes it wearisome.

Some change their philosophy of life with every book they read. One book sells them on Freud, the next on Marx; materialists one year, idealists the next; cynics for another period, and liberals for still another. They have their quivers full of arrows, but no fixed target. As no game makes the hunter tired of the sport, so the want of destiny makes the mind bored with life.

Boredom can lead to revolution. A boy is given a BB gun. If the father gives him a target, for example, a bull's-eye on the side of a barn or an old tin can, the boy is happy to shoot at it, and use his gun as it ought to be used. As soon as the target is rejected or ignored or not given, generally he goes in for shooting anything, particularly school windows. The revolutionary spirit in the world today is born of such purposeless and meaningless existence.

A university kept dogs for experimental purposes in two separate cages. In one cage were dogs without fleas; in the other were dogs with fleas who were waiting to be dipped and "defleaed." The professors noted that the dogs with fleas were more tranquil than the dogs without fleas, because they had something to keep them busy. The others howled and barked and in general created many problems of canine delinquency. The scientists concluded that physiological economy is directed to work and the expenditure of energy. The restlessness of the flealess dogs was a kind of regulatory mechanism for keeping the organism fit.

In the higher realms, human powers are directed to the expenditure of energy for an overall purpose; if a person lacks it, his or her giddiness and restlessness and consequent boredom are the price to pay. The most bored people in life are not the underprivileged but the overprivileged. The moral is not to have "fleas" or annoyances and troubles; but the moral is to have something to *do* and *live for,* not for today and tomorrow, but *always.*

When life has no intentional destiny; when it has no bivouac, no harbor, no ideal, it is full of mediocrity and tedium. It then becomes completely exteriorized, with consequent loss of much power and peace.

As Stephen Vincent Benét put it:

> Life is not lost by dying; Life is lost
> Minute by minute, day by dragging day,
> In all the thousand small uncaring ways.

Where there are no inner resources, but only staleness and flatness, such people say life has frustrated them: *No! They have frustrated life.* They excuse themselves saying they are bored because they are not loved: *No! They are bored because they do not love; because they have denied love....*

* * *

Many think, when we speak about a person's ultimate happiness as being union with God, that God is to be conceived as something extrinsic to us, as a kind of a pious "extra," or that God is related to us as a reward for a good life, or as a medal is related to study. A gold medal at the end of the school year is not intrinsically related to study. Many students do excellent work in school and get no medals. God and the happiness of heaven are not related to us that way. Rather, God and heaven are related to one another as blooming to a rose, or as a peach to a peach tree, or as an acorn to an oak, namely, as our intrinsic perfection without which we are incomplete, and with which we are happy.

It may be objected that there are people who are full of life who hate repetition; therefore, working toward the ideal goal is boring. No! Look at those who are full of life; they love repetition. Put a child on your knees and bounce it up and down two or three times; the child will say, "Do it again."

Or tell a child a funny story. I can remember my grandmother telling me the story of an Indian who came to kill a farmer who was splitting logs. The farmer induced the Indian to put his fingers in the split log for a second, which he did and was held prisoner. I never found out what happened to either the farmer or the Indian, but I said to her at least a thousand times, "Tell me again." The child never says, "That's an old story; I heard Uncle Ed tell it last week." The child says, "Tell me again." You blow smoke through your nose or you blow it through your ears, as I once thought an uncle could do, and the child will say, "Do it again."...

*   *   *

Because God is full of life, I imagine each morning Almighty God says to the sun, "Do it again"; and every evening to the moon and the stars, "Do it again"; and every springtime to the daisies, "Do it again"; and every time a child is born into the world asking for a curtain call, that the heart of the God might once more ring out in the heart of the babe....

Life is worth living when we live each day to become closer to God. When you have said your prayers, offered your actions in union with God, continue to enjoy the "thrill of monotony," and *Do it again!*

[LIFE IS WORTH LIVING]

Fatigue

T HE FATIGUE that concerns us presently is not physical fatigue, but rather mental fatigue. Why is there so much apathy and dullness and indifference in the world, and such a want of fire and enthusiasm? Why do so many say of life, "I can't stand it any longer; it's too much for me"?

There are two explanations. One is the mechanical theory that holds that everyone has a definite amount of energy, which is limited. Fatigue follows from too lavish an expenditure. Energy is very much like having money in the bank. If you draw too many checks on it, you become exhausted. Each person has a reservoir of energy that can be dissipated in a thousand channels. All fatigue on this theory is due to *exhaustion*.

The other theory might be called the "human" theory. It holds that if energy fails, it is not because the supply is used up, but because the channel is blocked, or because we did not use it properly. The chief cause of fatigue is not *exhaustion*, but *stagnation*. We are tired first in the mind, then in the body. Often it is the mind that makes the body tired. This demands an explanation of how the mind works.

The mind has two faculties. One faculty is the intellect, and the other faculty is the will. The faculty of intellect is for knowing; the faculty of the will is for choosing and doing. The object of the intellect is truth, and the object of the will is goodness or love. The will of itself is blind. The intellect or reason must lead the way. When the intellect

41

presents a goal, e.g., visit London, the will pays it the compliment of wishfulness. Nothing is desired unless it is known. The intellect gives us the target, and the will shoots the arrow. It is one thing to know the goal and quite another thing to work toward it. . . .

*   *   *

If there is no meaning to life, there is not much use in living.

There are three ways to achieve power and to overcome fatigue:

1. Have a master idea.

2. Strengthen the will.

3. Have recourse to outside power.

1. *A master idea.* The mind is strengthened by a strong idea. An English professor of psychiatry tested weight lifters. The three men averaged lifting 101 pounds. He hypnotized them and told them they were strong. They lifted 142 pounds, or almost 50 percent more weight. Because they got the idea of strength, they became strong. He hypnotized them again and told them that they were weak. They lifted only 29 pounds. The idea of weakness induced weakness in action. The mind was exhausted before the body. At the time of the San Francisco earthquake, thirty people who had been bedridden for thirty years got up and walked. The idea that they had to do something about their condition produced appropriate action. . . .

*   *   *

The first master idea to possess is to realize we were made for happiness. But in order to be happy, we have to satisfy the higher part of our being, namely, our intellect and our will. We strive for perfect truth and perfect love, which is God. The master idea then is that we are made to know, love, and serve God in this life and be happy with Him forever in the next. The body then becomes the servant of the mind, the senses minister to reason, and reason to faith. No one who loves this master idea is ever unhappy, even amid the trials and vicissitudes of life. Energy multiplies to achieve it, by goodness to neighbors, patience, charity, meekness, resignation, and some of the other forgotten virtues, like courtesy and sacrifice. Life becomes full of zeal, and even though sometimes one may do wrong, one nevertheless always has the map. There are many people who get off the road and stay off because they have no road map. As long as you have a master idea, you can get back. There are two classes of people in the world: those who fall down and those who stay down. A pig falls in the mud and stays in the mud; a lamb falls in the mud and gets out of the mud.

Strong reasons make strong actions. To occupy yourself with love of God and neighbor is never to be idle. Hell is full of the talented, but heaven, of the energetic. As sanctity declines, energy declines. Many today do not *believe* enough to be great. Mediocrity is the penalty for loss of faith.

2. *Strengthen the will.* Hardly ever does an educator today speak of training the will. A little boy asked his mother, "May I have another piece of cake?"

The mother said, "You have already had eight pieces."

"I know, Mother, but just let me have one more piece, please, please, please."

And the mother said, "All right."

Then the little boy said, "You haven't any willpower at all, have you?"

There is a world of difference between willing and wanting. Most people *want* to be good, but they do not *will* to be good. Augustine said, before he became a saint, "Dear Lord, I want to be pure; not now, but a little later on." That was before he became a saint! . . .

If people are told that they are animals or machines, they lose the sense of inner power to become better. A person is a slave of bad habit as long as he accepts the slavery. Why is it that those who constantly warn us of the danger of repressing our sex instincts never warn us about the danger of repressing our will to be better?

Character is like chiseling a statue; one has to knock off huge hunks of selfishness, which requires self-discipline. Only then does character begin to emerge. We mistakenly believe everything can be acquired without effort; for example, "How to learn French without studying vocabulary," or "How to learn to play the piano without reading notes," or "How to make money without working."

We never receive our second wind until we use up the first. God does not give us new graces until we exhaust ourselves in spending those already received. The condition of receiving new power is the resolute will to give power to others. We try to escape intellectual effort by reading picture magazines and novels exclusively and discover in the end that our power to think clearly has been lost. As George Bernard Shaw once said, "Our language is the language of Shakespeare, Thompson, and Milton, as we sit and croon like bilious pigeons."

Maybe our refusal to exercise our body could atrophy our muscles. Could the great increase of heart trouble be due to the fact that few exercise their hearts by hard exercise? I wonder if a ditchdigger ever developed angina pectoris? Maybe it is good for us that at our office and home we have to climb four flights of stairs for every meal.

Power is bought only in terms of willed service. Nonexpression of the will in effort and self-discipline has caused far more ravages than self-expression.

3. *Recourse to outside power.* The exercise of the will is right, but it is wrong if we think that we can do everything by our own will. We cannot lift ourselves by our own bootstraps or by the lobes of our ears. Those who rely only on their will generally become aggressive, domineering, self-willed, dictatorial, and proud. Human will has to depend on something else. The basic trouble with atheism is that it breathes the same air in that it breathes out.

There has to be another source of power outside our will. We do not nourish ourselves; we are dependent upon the plant and animal world outside. No organism is self-contained; it thrives only by contact with an environment that is nonself. We need air for our lungs and light for our eyes. When we are born, our mind is like our blackboard, on which nothing is written. Our five senses pour into the mind raw material, from which our intellect, like a great X ray, abstracts ideas, which we combine into judgments and reasoning processes.

Our spirits too are continuous with a larger spiritual world. We are not cisterns but wells; we grow less by our own power than by assimilation of outside forces. Our intellect and will both need to cooperate with this power of God. Once it gets into our intellect, it becomes faith; in our will, it becomes power. Divine energy of truth and love does not originate in us but flows through us. As we establish contact with the atmosphere, which cannot be seen or tasted by breathing, so we establish commerce with the divine source of power by prayer and the sevenfold channels that the good Lord Himself offers to our depleted human forces. Unite a dedicated will with this divine energy, and a character is transformed into inner peace and outer service.

[LIFE IS WORTH LIVING]

One basic reason for tiredness of mind is the conflict in all of us between ideal and achievement, between what we ought to be and what we are, between our longing and our having, between our powers of understanding and the incomprehensible mysteries of the universe.

[WAY TO HAPPINESS]

The Anatomy of Melancholy

MELANCHOLY IS SOMETHING so deep in our modern mood that its analysis should not be committed solely to the psychiatrist. It is not simply a disgust, or discontent, or sorrow, or even a suffering. In suffering, the emphasis is generally on external things and circumstances that make one sad; in melancholy, there is something interior that has been wounded, there is a kind of discontent of self, a hatred of being, a desire to be empty. Life almost turns against the very instinct of conservation and against legitimate self-love; there takes place a desire to empty oneself of all positive value, till one sinks into the emptiness and absurdity of life. Despair is like a child who, when you take away one of his playthings, throws the rest into the fire in his rage. Despair grows angry with itself, it turns on itself as its own executioner to revenge its misfortune, refuses to live under disappointments and crosses, and would rather not be at all than to be without the thing that it once imagined necessary for happiness.

Melancholy develops through three stages:

1. Egotism, or the affirmation of the self as an absolute

2. A sting of conscience, causing a hatred of goodness

3. A preoccupation with death, sometimes ending in suicide

1. *Egotism*. Melancholy is not just selfishness; it is a perpetual self-reverence and self-worship that refuses to recognize anything in the universe higher than itself. Perhaps without ever saying so, it boasts that it is its own law, its own truth, its own goodness, its own savior. The ego becomes a kind of closed circle; all objectivity is denied, such as neighbor and law, whether human or divine. Hence, there is no standard outside of the self, and no responsibility. Without a yardstick to measure the cloth of life, a yard is whatever one decides to be a yard. A false relationship to reality results, which is the characteristic of all neuroses.

Dostoevsky, the great Russian novelist of the last century, in an epilogue to *Crime and Punishment* speaks of personality imprisoned in subjectivist solitude, falling victim to the vainglorious delusion that it is dependent upon nothing. He speaks of it in terms of a "new unprecedented terrible pestilence" that arises from the depths of Asia and is spreading over the world; it is a germ that affects intellects and wills rather than the body.

Never before had men thought themselves so clever, never before had they believed so unshakably in their own wisdom, as did these creatures. Never before had men been so deeply convinced of the infallibility of their judgments, doctrines and principles; whole districts, whole cities, whole nations caught the infection, and behaved like madmen. Everybody was in a state of high excitement, and nobody understood anyone else; each one thought that he alone was in possession of the truth, and was deeply distressed — beating his breasts, weeping and wringing his hands — at the sight of his countrymen. Nobody knew on whom judgment should be passed or what sort of judgment it should be; no two people could agree as to what was good or what was bad — who should be prosecuted or who should be acquitted... in the cities alarm signals were given all day long; everyone answered summonses to mass meetings — but who had summoned them, and for what purpose? Nobody knew! Ordinary trades were abandoned because everybody had his own suggestions for improving them and no two people could agree. Agriculture was at a standstill.

In the whole world only a few people could save themselves; these were the pure elect, chosen to found a new human race, to create a new life, to renew and purify the world, but nobody noticed these people; nobody listened to their word or even heard their voices.

One meets the same spirit of egotism in Sartre, who says everything opposite me is non-me. What is non-me is nothing. I am the absolute; my neighbor is hell. A German philosopher in the same spirit of egotism said that if it could be mathematically proved and with absolute certitude that God exists, I would still reject His existence because He would set a limit to my ego. "Thy will be done" becomes "my will be done."

This is the first step in melancholy: a person declaring himself the absolute and unconditioned, setting himself up as God, and locking himself up in the narrow confines of his own finite limited being.

2. *The sting of conscience leading to hatred of goodness.* Egotism says, "I am not responsible for my actions." This assumes that a human being is only an animal and any sense of guilt is "morbid." But this necessarily involves the repressing of a sense of guilt into the unconsciousness. Though guilt is denied in consciousness, it is submerged into unconsciousness, where it comes out in two ways:

a. By an inner self-punishment, which not only anticipates unhappy outcomes but behaves as if the blow had already fallen; this is enjoyed in an unconsciously masochistic way. Associated with it is a love of seeing violence done to others; the punishment that one deserves is vicariously received by another. A love of horror movies and stories of violence done to another relieves for a time the need of atoning for the guilt.

b. A more important phase is when the melancholic becomes so depraved as to be insulted by virtues. It is a matter of the utmost necessity

for such a person to besmirch purity. What makes it all the more terrible is that the virtuous seem to be above insults. One of Dostoevsky's
characters, Versilov, insults the virtuous, thinking that by doing so he
will recover his integrity. He sees on the table an icon, the symbol of
goodness and morality. He first admits that he is split inside. "Do you
know that I feel as though I was split in two!" He looks around at all
with a serious face and a perfectly genuine candor. "Yes, I really feel
split in two mentally and I am horribly afraid of it. It is just as though
one's second half were standing beside one; there is the sensible and
rational self, but the other self is impelled to do something perfectly
senseless, and something very funny; and suddenly you notice that you
are longing to do that amusing thing, goodness knows why. You want
to, as it were, against your will; and though you fight against it with
all your might, you still want to. I once knew a doctor who suddenly
began whistling in church at his father's funeral. I really was afraid to
come to the funeral today, because, for some reason, I was possessed by
a firm conviction that I should begin to whistle or laugh in church, like
that unfortunate doctor who came to rather a bad end. . . . I really don't
know why, but I have been haunted by the thought of that doctor all
day; I am so haunted by it that I can't shake him off. Do you know,
Sonia, here I have taken up the icon again [he has picked it up and is
turning it about in his hand], and do you know that I have a dread-
ful longing now, this very second, to smash it against a stone, against
this corner, I am sure it would break in two halves — neither more
nor less." Versilov at this very moment puts his words into action. He
smashes the image, and it breaks in two — in exactly two pieces.

A person cannot escape what he is flying from. Guilt pursues that
person almost like a shadow. He reaches a point where he is no longer
a bad person but an evil person. A bad person will do wrong things,
such things as cheat, steal, slander, murder, and violate, but will still
admit the law. He will get off the road, but he will not throw away the
road map. An evil person, on the contrary, may not do any of these
bad things; he or she is concerned not with the concrete but with the
abstract. Such a person's desire is to completely destroy goodness, re-

ligion, morality, in a mad bigotry. He would justify in his life the false
desire of Nietzsche: "Evil be thou my good." Such a person seeks for a
transvaluation of values in which night is day and day is night, good is
evil and evil good.

When a person becomes conscious of the fact that he is a creature
of sin, he can react to it in one of two ways: by accepting the humiliation and making it the cornerstone of salvation, or by *revolt*. In the
first, through humility he discovers within himself the disfigured image
of Christ. In the second, he reacts against his depravity by seeking to
humiliate others as he himself has been humiliated. From that moment
on, any kind of virtue, or beauty, or nobility, is both desirable and hateful — desirable because one cannot destroy the divine image, hateful
because one wills not to possess it. Melancholics cannot touch anything without spoiling it. They want to spoil things because then they
can stop loving them; melancholics imagine that they would then be
reconciled with themselves.

3. *Preoccupation with death and, in some cases, suicide.* There is a fear
of death that is normal. This fear comes from the moral fact that we
know we ought not to die. Somehow we have a suspicion that it was
not part of the original plan for us. In a melancholic, however, there is
an abnormal fear of death, and an abnormal love of it. The abnormal
desire for it is in part caused by the fact that the melancholic has no
unified philosophy of life; he or she is very much like a planet that
has wandered out of its orbit; nothing but eccentricity, confusion, and
fission reigns in the person's mental life. This confusion, disaggregation,
and disillusion make for a desire for dismemberment, multiplicity, and
death. The second reason is that there is already a conflict within the
self that is self-destroying. There is a hatred of self, an inability to live
with self. When someone does wrong, he will pound his breast as if to
drive out the guilt. After the Crucifixion, those who witnessed it came
down from Calvary beating their breasts as if they would expunge from
their hearts the guilt within. This beating of the breast can reach a
point where there is a desire even to beat life out of self — which is
suicide.

Suicide is the final delirium of subjectivity, the annihilation of objectivity. A suicidal person refuses to live for the flowers, for the birds, for people, for children, even for God; it as though he or she were destroying by suicide the very things that irritated him or her — things on the outside that he or she could not control. Suicide is the ending of the subjective life without waiting for the objective. The "I" alone is the lord of life and death.

Suicidism has become a mental epidemic and a plague. It is not just because of unbearable misery, because for every one case in which there is poverty and need, there are numerous others in which people go through unbelievable misery and still want to live. It is not so often the underprivileged as the overprivileged who take their lives in a final dose of melancholy. An alcoholic often contemplates suicide. Suicide is like a chess player who cannot solve a problem before him, so he sweeps the pieces off the board. As this is no solution of the chess problem, a suicide is no solution of the problem of life. Animals do not commit suicide. It is only the eternal that can make a person despair. Despair is the absolute extreme of self-love. It turns its back on all others. In the end it is so disgusted with itself, it desires to be self-empty.

What makes our age sad is not that our joys have ceased, but our hopes have ceased. Hopes today are at a discount. It is security rather than happiness that seems to be the goal of modern life. We are like passengers who, taking a trip to sea, search not for the cabins but for the lifeboats. There is something psychologically profound in the custom of putting safety belts in automobiles to offer safety in times of wreck. Our melancholic age is looking forward to disaster even when on a pleasure trip. Despair is born of the meaninglessness of life. Whoever has a reason for living will endure anything. A starving person generally will not commit suicide, because of the desire that he has for life. Men and women in concentration camps endured the most intense suffering because they loved their faith or their country and their families; endurance, not despair, inspired them to live.

Melancholy, however, is not to be dismissed as absolute hopelessness so long as there is life. One can just as well start the road to ordered living with despair as with anything else. It happens that the modern person is not going to God through nature; he is not moved to the existence of God by a rational study of the order in nature, from which he concludes an intelligent Creator. Rather, he is moved to start with the disorder, the chaos, the misery, the unhappiness, in his own soul. Philosophers and psychologists must start with the person as he or she is, not as they would like to find that person.

If melancholy, boredom, and an uneasy, disturbed conscience be the condition of modern humanity, then one must start there. Despair can be of two kinds. One is *pessimistic despair*, resulting from one's refusal to seek the purpose of life. The other is a *creative despair*, in which one realizes one's inability to achieve peace through one's own efforts. His defeat and failure are his surest hope, provided he looks outside himself. Creative despair is the basis of the words of the Psalmist, *De profundis clamavi ad te, Domine.* It is the creative despair of a sick person in the face of a physician who heals, or the creative despair of an ignorant person before a master willing to teach. In creative despair, abyss cries out to abyss. On the one hand, there is the abyss of misery; on the other, the abyss of mercy; the emptiness of humanity, and the goodness of God. Whoever has misery without mercy is in despair. Whoever knows mercy without his own misery is proud and arrogant.

In creative despair, one begins with the inner tragedy of human existence, perceiving the contradiction that exists between what one is and what one ought to be. One sees a kind of cross in which the upright bar of life is contradicted by the horizontal bar of death. There is misery because one sees oneself traveling in four directions, *backward*, toward one's past and failures; *forward*, in an unknown future without a guide; *inward*, to a self that is already a kind of snake pit; and *outward*, toward things some of which we love, others of which we ignore, and others of which we fight against. No one can move in all four directions at once — hence indecision. The cross, therefore, is the perfect symbol of the abyss of misery, a sign of contradiction, frustration at the very heart of life.

The other abyss is mercy, not the mercy of a God who cannot understand human woe and suffering, but of a God Who emptied Himself of glory in order to take on the failings of humanity. A God Who in human form tasted the fears and the melancholies and despairs as He drank of the dark chalice in the Garden of Gethsemane; a God Who, in human form, took upon Himself all the sins of the world and, because He was sinless, could act as the Intercessor for all those in misery, saying, "Father, forgive them for they know not what they do."

[LIFE IS WORTH LIVING]

Darkness may be creative, for it is there that God plants His seeds to grow and his bulbs to flower. It is at night that the sheep that are scattered are gathered into the unity of the sheepfold, when the children come home to their mother and the soul back again to God. Daylight deceives us, but as we awake at night, we get a new sense of values; darkness seems to tell the awful truth. As the psalmist put it: "Day to day pours forth speech and night to night declares knowledge" (Ps 19:2). Night has its wonders, as well as day; darkness is not final, except to those who are without God.

[CROSS-WAYS]

Love's Overflow

WHY DID GOD create a world? God created the world for something like the same reason that we find it hard to keep a secret! Good things are hard to keep. The rose is good, and tells its secret in perfume. The sun is good, and tells its secret in light and heat. Humanity is good, and tells the secret of its goodness in the language of thought. But God is infinitely good, and therefore infinitely loving. Why therefore could not He by a free impulse of His love let love overflow and bring new worlds into being? God could not keep, as it were, the secret of His love, and the telling of it was creation.

Love overflowed; eternity moved and said to time, "Begin." Omnipotence moved and said to nothingness, "Be." Light moved and said to darkness, "Be light." Out from the fingertips of God there tumbled planets and worlds. Stars were thrown into their orbits and the spheres into space. Orbs and families of orbs began to fill the heavens. The great march of the world began, in which planet passes by planet and sphere by sphere, without ever a hitch or a halt. In that long procession of the unfolding of the creative power of God, there came first matter, then palpitating life and the paradise of creation with its fourfold rivers flowing through all lands rich with gold and onyx, and finally those creatures made not by a *Fiat* but by a council of the Trinity — the first man and woman.

Quite naturally the mind of that Great Architect might have conceived ten thousand other possible worlds than this. This is not absolutely the best world that God could have made. But it is the best world for the purpose that He had in mind in making it. Almighty God chose to make a universe in which not all the creatures would be like sticks and stones, trees and beasts, each of which is impelled by a law of nature, or a law of instinct, to a determined rigorous end, without the slightest enjoyment of freedom. He willed to place in paradise a creature made to His own image and likeness, but a creature different from all others, because endowed with that glorious gift of freedom, which is the power of saying "Yes" or "No," of choosing to sacrifice oneself to duty or duty to oneself, and forever remaining master and captain of one's own fate and destiny. In other words, God willed to make a moral universe, and the only condition upon which morality is possible is freedom.

In the very nature of things, ethics and morality can exist only upon the condition of a veto. Bravery, for example, is possible only in a world in which a person may be a coward. Virtue is possible only in a world where a person may be vicious. Sacrifice is possible only in that order in which a person may be selfish. Love is possible only when it is possible not to love. Cold statues cannot love. It is the possibility of saying "No" that gives so much charm to the heart when it says "Yes." A victory may be celebrated only on those fields in which a battle may be lost. Hence, in the divine order of things, God made a world in which man and woman would rise to moral heights, not by that blind driving power that makes the sun rise each morning, but rather by the exercise of that freedom in which one may fight the good fight and enjoy the spoils of victory, for no one shall be crowned unless he has struggled....

God willed to give to the first man and woman certain gifts that would be theirs permanently, and for their posterity, providing that they proved faithful in their love. Among these gifts were immunity from disease and death, freedom from the rebellion of flesh over reason, and above all a gift of *knowledge* that far surpassed reason and enabled them to grasp divine truths in a far greater way than a telescope reveals to the eye the distant stars and planets; and a gift of *power* or *grace* that made the first man and woman not mere creatures of the handiwork of God, but God's own children, and co-heirs with Him in the Kingdom of Heaven. These gifts, be it understood, were even less due to the nature of man than the power of blooming belongs to marble, or the song of a poet belongs to a beast.

But these gifts were conditioned, for the universe is moral. They could be kept on one condition, namely, by loving God, and loving God means loving what is best for ourselves. But how try Love? The only way to try love is in a trial that forces one to declare it. The only way for Adam and Eve as free moral beings to prove their love and gratitude to God was by choosing Him in preference to all else, and admitting that their added knowledge and their added power or grace were gifts. A double condition was laid upon them to test their love.

The first part of the condition was *obscure*; it gave them an opportunity to admit that the added knowledge was a gift of God. The second part was *reserved*; it allowed them to admit that the added power of the will was a gift of God. Thus they would show that they loved God with their whole mind and their whole will, and preferred Him to all things else. In concrete terms, the trial was that they might enjoy all the riches of the garden of paradise; but the fruit of one tree — the tree of the knowledge of good and evil — they were not to touch. God did not say *why* they should not — and that was the *obscure* point on which their intelligence was tried. We should believe God on this point as on all others. God *did* say they must abstain from the fruits of that tree. That was the *reserved* point that was the trial of their will. God was imposing a limit to the sovereignty of humans, reminding them that if they did the one thing forbidden they would imperil all the things provided, and that, like Pandora later on, if they should open the forbidden box, they would lose their treasures and let loose on the world confusion worse confounded.

The story of the Fall as recorded in Genesis is known to all. Satan, appearing in the form of a serpent, tempted Eve with the question that destroyed confidence, which is the root of all love. "Why has God commanded you that you should not eat of every tree of Paradise?" (Gen 3:1). Eve looks at the forbidden fruit; it is beautiful to behold. More and more she turns herself from the voice and thought of God to the fragrancy and imagined sweetness of the forbidden fruit. The lingering thought passes into a vivid imagination, the vivid imagination into a burning wish, the burning wish into a half-formed purpose, the half-formed purpose into a hasty act. Swiftly the crisis is upon her, as all such crises are, and the deed was done irrevocably until time shall be no more.

She gave the forbidden fruit to Adam, and pride and self-will entered into his heart. He wanted to show he *did know* what was good for him, and that his mind need not be kept obscured on any one point, nor his will reserved by any one condition. He wanted to be independent and show that he could do what he liked. And so he ate the fruit that he was forbidden to eat, because it was fair, and still more to show his own independence. Surely, this is understandable. Have we not done the same thing in our own lives over and over again? When we were children, were we not forbidden to do something that we wished to do? Did we not long for it and determine to have it all the more because it was forbidden? Adam did it for the very same reason, and that act of disobedience by which Adam failed the test of love is the first sin of this created universe, the sin that infected humanity in its origin and the sin that, for that reason, has been called original sin.

The whole trial was perfectly reasonable. Imagine a wealthy man who owns a beautiful estate. He tells his chauffeur and the chauffeur's wife that he will permit them to live in his mansion, ride in his limousines, use his servants, enjoy his yacht, play about his spacious gardens, eat at his expense. In a word, they are to enjoy everything, provided that they will not touch a certain oil painting that hangs in one of his drawing rooms.... By doing the one thing forbidden, they would lose all the privileges provided, and who would accuse the master of the house of injustice if he no longer permitted them to enjoy his gifts?

The doctrine, then, of the Fall is far from the travesty made upon it by frivolous minds who make the ordinance of God repose solely on an apple, for to do this is to miss the point of the whole story. To speak of the Fall does not mean merely a garden and a serpent; to say that it is much more than any garden or any snake is not the same as saying there was no garden and there was no snake. It is simply saying what is of primary and what is of secondary importance; what is primary is the respect due to God, the fruit of the tree being the symbol of that respect. To make light of the fruit of a tree under such circumstances is just as rash as to make light of the flag of our country, as a symbol of our country's sovereignty. A flag stands for a nation, and the hand that carries it would retain it at the cost of a thousand deaths rather than let it be seized and desecrated by the enemy. It may be a small thing to violate a cloth that is red and white and blue, but it is no small thing to desecrate that for which it stands.

So, likewise, in the terrestrial paradise, the famous tree in which God summarized all the knowledge of good and evil was a symbol, a moral limit that God imposed on the sovereignty of man and woman to prove their obedience and love. To say it was only a fable is to miss the great truth that things — a handshake or a smile, for example — may not only be but may also signify.

[The Divine Romance]

Agnosticism

GNOSTICISM IS AN EVIL when it contends not only that an individual mind knows nothing, but also that no other mind knows anything. In this sense it is cowardly, because it runs away from the problems of life. Only about 10 percent of the people think for themselves. Columnists and headline writers think for the greater percent of the remainder. Those who are left are the agnostics, who think agnosticism is an answer to the riddle of life. Agnosticism is not an answer. It is not even a question.

There is, however, a sense in which agnosticism is desirable. In fact, a healthy agnosticism is the condition of increase of knowledge. A person may be agnostic in one of two ways, either by doubting the value of things *below* him in dignity, or by doubting the value of things *above* him in dignity. Modern agnosticism doubts the things *above* a person and hence ends in despair; Christian agnosticism doubts the value of things *below* a person and hence ends in hope.

These statements admit of universal application. The universe may be compared to a temple made up of a vestibule, a sanctuary, and a Holy of Holies. Josephus in his "Antiquities" tells us that it was Jewish belief that the temple of Jerusalem with its three divisions was modeled on the plan upon which God built the universe, which too had its vestibule, its sanctuary, and its Holy of Holies.

The vestibule of creation or the material world is the world of the sun, moon, stars, plants, animals, and humans — in a word, every sensible thing. The sanctuary of creation is the world of causes, of science, philosophy, and natural law. The Holy of Holies of creation is the world of mystery and revelation, such as the Trinity and the Incarnation. The same key that unlocks the vestibule of creation does not unlock the sanctuary of creation nor does the world of causes open the Holy of Holies. There are three keys for the temple. The first key that unlocks the world of matter is the five senses, by which we taste, see, touch, smell, and hear the material world and thus enter into communion with it. The second key that unlocks the world of causes, of purposes, is the key of reason, which enables us to penetrate the inner meaning and purpose of things. Finally, the key that unlocks the Holy of Holies of creation is the delicate key of faith.

Although there are three keys for this temple, we must not think that one part of it is opposed to the other. As a matter of fact, we go from the vestibule of creation to the sanctuary and from the sanctuary to the Holy of Holies by exactly the same kind of mental attitude, and that is the attitude of agnosticism. We may doubt one of two things, it was said above: either the value of things that are above us or the value of things that are below us. Modern skepticism doubts the value of things that are above us, such as grace, the divinity of Christ, the Trinity, and the perfection of humanity by a gift of God. But to doubt these things is to put an obstacle to progress and a bar to upward growth. This kind of agnosticism or even skepticism is really a species of septic poisoning.

The other kind of doubt that doubts the value of things that are below — that is, the human power to save oneself, the possibility of this world's giving complete happiness, the capacity of science to satisfy the human heart completely — is to make a person higher than this world and to open the path for further progress and perfection. To return to the point, I say that that process by which we pass from the vestibule to the sanctuary and from the sanctuary to the Holy of Holies of creation is by the latter kind of doubt or agnosticism.

There are then three sources of vision in this universe, each different in kind and yet each the perfection of the other: the eye, the reason, and faith. The first unlocks the vestibule of creation or the material universe; the second unlocks the sanctuary of creation or the world of causes and finalities in the natural order; the third unlocks the Holy of Holies or the world of Incarnation and grace. Observe now, how each reaches its perfection, namely, by a healthy agnosticism — an act of humility or a doubt. In other words, the ascent from the vestibule to the sanctuary, from the sanctuary to the Holy of Holies, is made thanks to a doubt. First of all, note that the eye is never constantly looking out on the material universe. It does not always enjoy the clear vision of the sunlight, even when the sun is shining. Every now and then it must go into temporary darkness; every now and then it must have a doubt about its vision; every now and then it must be skeptical — and its skepticism is a wink. After the wink it opens itself and sees better; that is why light always seems doubly strong when we come out of a cave.

Reason too must follow the same law under the penalty of never coming to a clear vision and understanding of things. In moments of intense intellectual concentration we sometimes shut our eyes, bolt up the doors of sense-knowledge, in order that we may the more clearly bask in the light of reason. As the eye shuts out the light of day to enjoy it better the next moment, so the reason shuts out the light of mere experimental sense-knowledge in order that it may more clearly rejoice in the light of the mind. The *doubt* about the conclusiveness of material vision of the universe is the *wink* of reason, its momentary death to a lower life as a prelude to the riches of a higher one. The light of the intellect never shines so brightly as at the moment when it winks on the world of sense, but that doubt does not destroy the lower kind of vision, for when we have solved our intellectual problem in the sanctuary of our mind, we can open the doors of the senses once more, and for some very mysterious reason the eye sees things differently — "in a new light," as we often put it.

Now what holds true of the eye and mind holds true of faith or the great world of the Incarnation continued by progressive filiation. How can we come to that full-orbed vision of faith? By no other means than by following what seems to be the most natural thing in the world — that restful act of winking — winking on reason, pulling down its shutters for a brief moment; in other words, doubting that reason can and does know all things knowable. This kind of wink is the most difficult of all; the very prospect of doing it makes us afraid that we may lose our reason, or go blind intellectually, but this is a groundless fear. The eye did not go blind because it winked on daylight, neither will the intellect go blind because it winks on science or reason. What will happen will be an improvement in the clarity of intellectual vision, an enlargement of its field and range, faith being to reason what a telescope is to the eye.

It is during that first terrible moment of doubt about reason, that plaintive admission of healthy skepticism, "Help thou my unbelief," that God sends His gifts of faith and grace. Never once does this outlook on knowledge ask us to pluck out our eyes, or to extinguish the light of our reason. It asks us to use our reason, to use that first, to use it hard, to investigate divine claims, but not to believe that reason can give the answer to all life's riddles. After a study, then a wink, then a doubt about the finality of reason, then a suspicion that there is a higher light, and then, aided by grace, the ascent to faith. Once on those heights, then open the eyes, call up reason, verify, understand, and apply those mysteries of faith to the world of reason and sense. And so little by little new vistas of truth will open up, and what were even natural mysteries before will now glow with a new brilliance. Thus faith is interpreted sometimes by reason, and reason holds up the hands of faith until that last great temporary wink comes in the sleep of death, when we reopen our eyes to the unveiled vision of the Truth, which is God, the Light that is so bright that a celestial Jerusalem needs not a sun, for the sun is the light of His face.

This brings us back to our starting point. The learned gentry of our modern world are unlearned because they never have a doubt. They try to make everything clear, and hence make everything mysterious. They forget that even nature has a mystery; that there is something in this great cosmos of ours that is just so terribly mysterious that we cannot "see" it, and that is the sun. It makes us wink whether we like it or not, and yet, in the light of that great natural mystery everything else in the world becomes clear. So too in higher realms, it is in the light of such a great supernatural mystery as the Incarnation that all things become clear, even the problem of evil.

[OLD ERRORS AND NEW LABELS]

Broadmindedness, which sacrifices principles to whims, dissolves entities into environment, and reduces truth to opinion, is an unmistakable sign of the decay of the logical faculty.

[MOODS AND TRUTHS]

Fingers, Hands, and Nails

THE FIRST APPEARANCE of Our Lord in the Upper Room was to only ten of the Apostles; Thomas was not present. He was not with the Apostles, but the gospel assumes that he should have been with them. The reason of his absence is unknown; but likely it was because of his unbelief. In three different passages of the gospel, Thomas is always portrayed as looking on the darker side of things, as regards both the present and the future. When the news came to Our Lord about the death of Lazarus, Thomas wanted to go and to die with him. Later on, when Our Blessed Lord said that He would return again to the Father and prepare a place for His Apostles, Thomas' doleful answer was that he knew not where the Lord was going, nor did he himself know the way.

Immediately after the other Apostles became convinced of the Resurrection and glory of Our Divine Savior, they brought to Thomas the tidings of the Resurrection. Thomas did not say he refused to believe, but that he was unable to believe until he had some experimental proof of the Resurrection, in spite of their testimony that they had seen the Risen Lord. He enumerated the conditions of his belief:

Unless I see the mark of the nails on his hands, unless I put my finger into the place where the nails were, and my hands into his side, I will not believe it. (Jn 20:25)

The disparity between those who believed and those who were unprepared for belief could be seen in the reception that the ten got as they told Thomas of the Resurrection. His refusal to trust the testimony of ten competent companions, who had seen the Risen Christ with their own eyes, proved how skeptical was the gloomy man. His, however, was not the frivolous skepticism of indifference or hostility to truth; he wanted knowledge in order to have faith. It was unlike the self-wise who want knowledge against faith. In one sense, his attitude was that of the scientific theologian who promotes knowledge and intelligence after having banished all doubt....

*   *   *

There are some who will not believe even when they see, such as Pharaoh; others believe only when they see. Above both these types the Lord God placed those who had not seen and yet believed. Noah had been warned by God of the things that had not yet come to pass; he believed as he prepared his ark. Abraham went out of his own home not knowing whither he went, but still trusting in the God who promised that he would be the father of a progeny more numerous than the sands of the seas. If Thomas had believed through the testimony of his fellow disciples, his faith in Christ would have been greater; for Thomas had often heard his Lord say that He would be crucified and rise again. He also knew from the Scriptures that the Crucifixion was the fulfillment of a prophecy, but he wanted the additional testimony of the senses.

Thomas thought that he was doing the right thing in demanding the full evidence of sensible proof; but what would become of future generations if the same evidence was to be demanded by them? The future believers, the Lord implied, must accept the fact of the Resurrection from those who had been with Him. Our Lord thus pictured the faith of believers after the apostolic age when there would be none

who would have seen it; but their faith would have a foundation because the Apostles themselves had seen the Risen Christ. They saw
that the faithful might be able to do so without seeing, believing on
their testimony. The Apostles were happy, not just because they had
seen Our Lord and believed; they were far happier when they fully
understood the mystery of Redemption and so lived in it, and even
had their throats cut for the reality of the Resurrection.

Some gratitude must always, however, be credited to Thomas, who
touched Christ as a man but believed in Him as God.

[LIFE OF CHRIST]

What is tolerance? Tolerance is an attitude of reasoned
patience toward evil, and a forbearance that restrains us
from showing anger or inflicting punishment. But what is
more important than the definition is the field of its application. The important point here is this: Tolerance applies
only to persons, but never to truth. Intolerance applies
only to truth, but never to persons. Tolerance applies to
the erring; intolerance to the error.

[OLD ERRORS AND NEW LABELS]

Ethics for the Unethical

THERE SHOULD BE a vacation for certain overworked words, and in particular the word "crisis." What "service" is to a Kiwanis booster, the word "crisis" is to moralists. This latter class have used it so often as to prove without doubt that Stevenson was right in saying that not by bread alone do men live but principally by catchwords. It is hardly possible to pick up a magazine today without reading an article by some self-styled ethicist on "The Crisis in Morals."

The repeated use of the word "crisis" in reference to morals is interesting, for it reveals a tendency on the part of many modern writers to blame the abstract when the concrete is really at fault. They speak, for example, of the problem of crime, rather than of the criminal; of the problem of poverty, rather than of the poor; and of the "crisis in morals," when really the crisis is among people who are not living morally. The crisis is not in ethics but in the unethical. The failure is not in the law, but in the law-breakers.

The truth of this observation is borne out by the failure of such writers to distinguish between the problem of making people conform to standards and that of making standards conform to people. Instead of urging people to pass the test, they alter the test. Instead of inspiring them to hold to their ideals, they change the ideals. In accordance with this logic, they urge that morals be changed to suit those who cannot live morally, and that ethics be changed to please those who cannot live ethically. All this takes place in accordance with the democratic principle of certain philosophers, who are prepared to construct any kind of philosophy that people desire. If we want ghosts, the democratic philosophers, who know the will of the populace, will write a philosophy justifying ghosts; if the man in the street wants to follow the line of least moral resistance, philosophers will develop for him the justifying philosophy of "self-expression"; if the person-about-town has no time for the thoughts of eternity, then philosophers develop for him or her the philosophy of "space-time."

There are ultimately only two possible adjustments in life: One is to suit our lives to principles; the other is to suit principles to our lives. "If we do not live as we think, we soon begin to think as we live." The method of adjusting moral principles to the way we live is just such a perversion of the due order of things. Just suppose this logic were applied in the classroom. Boys and girls find it difficult to spell "knapsack" and "pneumonia," because the spelling of these words is not in the line of least phonetic resistance. Others too find it very hard to learn the multiplication table. Many a budding liberal mathematician cannot crush the urge to say that three times three equals six. Now here is a real "crisis" in spelling and mathematics, a kind of intellectual anarchy much akin to the moral anarchy described by our intelligentsia. How meet the "crisis"? One way to meet it is the way to meet any crisis, that is, by criticism; the other way to meet it is to write a new speller and a new mathematics entitled "A Preface to Spelling" or "Crisis in Mathematics." This is precisely what has taken place in the field of morals. Instead of making people conform to principles of morality, they change the principles. This kind of philosophy would never have permitted the Prodigal Son to return to his father's house. It would have settled the "crisis" by finding a new and handsome name for the husks he was throwing to the swine, and called it "progress away from antiquated modes of morality."

All the books and articles on "the crisis in morality" touch on three points: the nature of morality, its origin, and its test. In discussing the general nature of morality, most authors reduce it to convention or taste. But before arriving at that conclusion, they seem to sense the inadequacy of the very solution they propose, and one of them makes this rather excellent observation: "Social conventions change: the particular actions calculated to suit them change with them, as, e.g., if the rule of the road were changed in England, we should drive on the right instead of the left. But the quality required for the right action does not change. It is just as important to drive carefully and considerately whatever the law of the road may be. The driver who says, 'First they say "left," then they say "right"; it is all a mess and I am free to be a road-hog' is indulging in a false argument."

So far, so good. But he immediately falls into the very logical pitfall he had asked others to avoid, for he makes two diametrically opposed moral principles akin to the convention of driving on the right or left side of the road. He writes: "So monogamy and polygamy are social conventions." In other words, for him there is no more difference between a moral system that permits a man to have one wife and a moral system that permits a man to have many wives, than there is between a traffic system that permits vehicles to drive on the right and another that permits vehicles to drive on the left. Now this is very poor logic. The difference between monogamy and polygamy is not the difference between the right side of the road and the left side of the road; it is a question of different roads, for monogamy is a one-road marriage, and polygamy is a boulevard. One could still be traveling in the proper direction whether he drove to the right as in America or to the left as in England. But he would not be doing so if he took an entirely different road, or a wrong road. Such is polygamy in relation to morality.

We agree with this philosopher in saying that this conclusion is false: "First they say 'left,' then they say 'right'; it is all a mess and I am free to be a road-hog." Why, then, does he, who makes morality a convention, consent to make a man a wife-hog, for such is what he does when he makes polygamy a matter of taste? If traffic laws and marriage laws are both conventions, why say the road-hog is wrong in one instance and not the wife-hog in the other instance? For the life of me, I cannot see why, if it is wrong to take up more than one-half the road, it is not also wrong or more wrong to take up more than one better-half. Such authors' moral traffic needs regulation, and needs it badly. . . .

*   *   *

Finally, the new philosophy of morality offers aesthetics or "fastidiousness" as the test of morality. "As far as I can analyze my own feelings," one writes, "I should say that the motive which keeps me from a bad action is a feeling that as I contemplate it I do not like the look of it or the smell of it. I feel it to be ugly or foul or not decent — not the sort of thing with which I want to be associated. And, similarly, the thing that nerves me toward a good but difficult action is a feeling that it seems beautiful or fine, the sort of thing that I love as I look at it and would like to have for my own."

Here there is the false equation between feeling good and being good, and between feeling bad and being bad. What is wrong is not considered wrong but ugly, and what is right is not considered right but beautiful. The Scholastics were fond of saying that there is no disputing about tastes. The new morality would make taste the ground and foundation of morality. But the test of "fastidiousness" and "aesthetics" for morality leaves no basis for obligation. How apply it to debts? Will the bills at the end of the month be paid according to the principles of aesthetics or the principles of justice? Will only those statements printed on beautiful parchment receive our attention, while those printed on yellow foolscap be left unpaid?

Suppose this test of morality were applied to international conflicts. According to its principles, it would be wrong to go to war with Turkey because one does not "like the looks of it," but it would be right to go to war with Switzerland because its Alpine heights are "beautiful." By the same aesthetic test, adultery would be wrong if Mr. Smith's wife had lost her "school-girl complexion," but would be right if she had the "skin you love to touch." Murder would be wrong only for the person who, "analyzing his feelings," admits he does not like "the smell of it," but it would be right for the one who reduced it to a fine art. What the new morality resolves itself into is this: You are wrong if you do a thing you do not feel like doing; and you are right if you do a thing you feel like doing. Such a morality is based not only on "fastidiousness," but on "facetiousness." The standard of morality then becomes the individual feeling of what is beautiful, instead of the rational estimate of what is right.

The "smell of a thing" may be a good test for garlic, but is not a good test for morality. "The sort of a thing that I love as I look at it" may be a good test for a sunset, but there can be no end to moral confusion worse confounded if it is going to justify a violation of the commandment, "Neither shall you covet your neighbor's wife" (Deut 5:21). In a word, the fundamental difficulty with this system of morals is that it is impossible to be wrong unless, perchance, one disagrees with its aesthetics....

*   *   *

If the nature of a person is rational, then one's natural tendencies must be judged rationally. But to judge anything rationally is to judge it in relation to the end or purpose for which it was created. A pen is to be judged by its capacity for writing, for that is why it was made; an eye is to be judged by its powers of vision, for that is the reason of its being. Human beings were made for a perfect fruition of their desire and striving for Life, Truth, and Love, which is God. We are, therefore, to be judged in relation to this end, that is, in our submission to or rebellion against it....

*   *   *

Morality, then, is order in relation to an end. And that all things might tend to their own proper destiny, Almighty God has placed in the various hierarchies of creation an immanent law to guide them. The laws of nature, such as gravitation, chemical affinity, and the like, direct the chemicals to the fulfillment of their natures. The laws of life, such as metabolism, guide plants to the perfection of their destiny. Instincts guide animals, and reason directs humans. The practical reason that enables a human being to fit particular cases under the general principles touching his or her final destiny is *conscience*.

Treasures of the Subconscious

H AS PSYCHOLOGY revealed totally the mystery of the sub-consciousness? Besides our libidinous instincts, repressed desires, drives to pleasure and sex, and the collective myths of our human ancestry, is there not another drive? Our consciousness and anthropology reveal a great treasure in the depths of our being. The subconsciousness need not be just a cesspool, something we are so ashamed of that it takes constant prodding to bring it to the surface; it is not always a sewerage and drainage system full of the muck and rot of our lives.

Besides the id there is another neglected area for which we have to find a name. Since Freud used the Latin word *id* to signify that cellar of repressed desires, we will use a Greek word *pneuma* to describe the other aspect, though we could use the Hebrew word *ruah.*

Both the id and the pneuma are in the subconscious levels of our mind; through them pass suggestions, desires, urges, drives, and impulsions that seek entrance into the conscious level of life and conduct. They are also the same in that there is a little censor at the top of the stairs who can keep down the dynamisms, drives, and thrusts of the pneuma if it does not like them. In fact, there are seven censors battling against the pneuma: egotism, lust, greed, anger, laziness, intemperance, and jealousy. But there is one big difference: The id is principally concerned with the drive to pleasure. The pneuma is concerned with a drive toward peace, harmony, integration, and happiness. There is in us a double drive: one toward giving release to our carnal nature, the other giving freedom to our deeper spiritual nature. One is an urge to flaunt conscience and the moral law and to be bad; the other is to grow in goodness and love of neighbor; one is to exalt our own ego, the other to serve neighbor and to crush our selfishness.

We are, therefore, solicited in two ways: one toward release of what is egotistic, the other toward a harmony and perfection of our nature. In other words, we are tempted also to be good.

How far we have gotten away from the total understanding of our subconscious mind will be clear from one word. When I say the word "temptation," what images and ideas are conjured up in your mind? "Engage in illicit sex"? "Get drunk"? "Rob"? "Steal"? and so on. Why do we always associate the word with what is rotten, immoral, or antisocial? Why does the subconsciousness always have to be considered a Gehenna or a drainage ditch? Why do we assume that every solicitation we have is something we would be ashamed to admit in polite society? Analyze yourself, and you will find this astounding fact: You have more temptations to be good than you have to be bad.

How many times have you been tempted to help a poor family, and how often have you felt sad if you did not and happy when you did? How often were you tempted to give up excessive drinking, bad temper, stealing, to "see what is in the Bible," to be kinder to your spouse, more gentle to your children, less cranky with your employees, less sarcastic to your neighbor, to try praying, to share your wealth with the hungry, to be more interested in community welfare? It is not only devils who walk up those stairs to the conscious mind; the stairs are really like Jacob's ladder with angels on every rung. And as regards repression, we knock more good thoughts over the head than we do bad thoughts. If, as some say, repression of our primitive instincts is wrong, why is not the repression of our meaningful instincts also wrong?

Why must we think of our subconscious always as a garbage pail instead of a dinner table? Why conceive that the energy of electric power is to give us a shock and not to light and heat? Are there only snakes underground, or do we also find gold? Do not the depths of the soil shoot up oil and fountains of water, as well as being the centers of earthquakes? The time has come when psychiatrists must see the subconscious not just as a mudhole where pigs love to wallow but also a runway where planes take off for a flight into the sky. The subconscious may be a basement, but it is one where we not only throw out refuse, but also keep our groceries, our hobbies, and our playroom and our wine.

What about the origin of this pneuma that transmits urges and drives from the subterranean part of our lives? Where does it come from? As psychiatrists say, the id has its origin outside us; so does the pneuma. The id, they say, is due either to contacts with our environment or more remotely with our animal ancestry, or it is cultural lag in the evolutionary process, a result of the collective unconsciousness of the race.

As the origin of the id is external — that is, not wholly of our making — and yet that through which all our drives function, so the origin of the pneuma is external, even much more so, though it too functions through our subconsciousness. In fact, it is very mysterious, something like the wind, which is invisible and yet strong. We pass over naming the source of the pneuma to concentrate on its silent, enigmatical intrusion into our subconsciousness.

How often we have been moved by an inspiration to change our lives; we know that it does not come from ourselves, for when we have it, we say, "I don't know what made me do this." A truck driver in Los Angeles, speeding down a highway, saw a large paper carton ahead of him. Generally, he said, he would drive over it and crush it, for it gave him a sense of power. But this time, he suddenly swerved to avoid it, stopped, got out of his truck cab, and went back to take it off the highway. Lo and behold, it was moving! A little boy had crawled into it and was propelling himself across the road. When asked what made him do it, the driver answered, "God! Because I never acted that way before."

How often a soldier in battle will be suddenly inspired to crawl out of a trench in the face of murderous shellfire to rescue a wounded buddy in a veritable no-man's-land. Braver than ever before in his life, he is praised for his rescue but will disdain it, saying, "Anyone else would have done it. I deserve no credit." In other words, "I did not do it — *something else moved me.*"

A characteristic of the upsurgence of the subconscious mind is what might be called sensing a crisis. H. G. Wells expressed it well: "At times in the silence of the night, and in rare lonely moments, I come upon a sort of communion of myself and something great that is not myself...it takes on the effect of a sympathetic person and my communion has a quality of fearless worship." What is present is a kind of dissolving of the elements of consciousness, as if some new chemical had been poured into the soul, and there begins to be a surrender to what the individual believes to be a higher power.

Thus there pass through the subconscious mind inspirations, insights, new values, and motivations that never before were entertained. They did not come from ourselves, and if we correspond with them, they completely remake us. They change fear into love, indifference into enthusiasm, hate into service. This *pneuma does not belong to our nature as such*, though the id does. But it is so constantly introduced into our impoverished nature that it seems to be a part of our life. When it touches us, it seems to affect principally our intellect and our will: the intellect, by enlightening us to see a truth we never saw before, and our will by giving us a power to do something we never had the strength to do before.

But the healing and elevating power of the pneuma always sets up a counterresistance on the part of our disordered human condition. We are not easily persuaded to give up our sinking ship. The id revolts against the pneuma and the pneuma against the id, making our heart the battleground. The egotistic self is threatened with its conceits, lusts, intemperance, anger, and the like. To die to them is not easy, even though the prospect of peace is so appealing and desirable. But once the pneuma is at the helm of the ship, the psychic regions are filled with an indescribable joy and delight.

Just as not everyone gives way to the sexual license that the id may suggest, so not everyone accepts the temptation of the pneuma to re-organize one's life. But when one does, among many effects that might be mentioned we concentrate on but one — a complete change of life's direction.

If I take a ball and roll it across the floor, it will move in one direc-tion unless diverted by a superior power. So too our lives very quickly become grooved through habit. They will roll by mere inertia in that same direction of crime, insensibility, mediocrity, emptiness, banality, unless some outside power or force alters their direction.

A law runs through nature that the lower is taken up into the higher. Chemicals are taken up into plants, plants into animals, and animals into man. Everywhere there is an upsurge to life. Lower life is meant to be born to a higher life. But there is one condition — the carbons, phosphates, oxygen, nitrogen, and other chemicals are never privileged to live in a plant kingdom, unless two things happen: The plant must intercept them, incorporate them into itself, and the chem-icals, in their turn, must die to their lower nature. It is as if the grass and the trees and the roses said to the chemicals, "Unless you die to yourself, you cannot live in my kingdom. You must be reborn from above" (Jn 3:3).

Plants, in their turn, can become one with the sentient, mobile life of the animal, if the animal comes down to them, descends to their lower life, and takes them up into itself. The plant, in its turn, must be pulled up from the roots. The same is true of the lower orders living in our body — to become one with the living, thinking, loving being, man must humble himself and go down to their lower state; they in turn must submit to the sacrifice of the knife and the fire, and thus the law is fulfilled: "Unless you die to yourself you cannot live in my kingdom. You must be born again from above" (Jn 3:3).

Now the pneuma that works inside us is a summoning presence, a kind of alien intruder, but one that always respects our freedom. Animals do not consult plants or carry on a dialogue with them before using them as food. But the pneuma does not violently possess us; it solicits quietly, it tempts, it leads us into a desert, it begs us to die to what is lower. Once we freely consent to absorb the élan and drive of the pneuma, there is a peace that the world cannot give and a joy that surpasses all understanding. Most of us miss the exhilaration, because we prefer to move in the horizontal areas of monotony instead of the vertical heights where there is new knowledge and deeper love.

There is not a single person in the world who has not experienced both the id and the pneuma, though greater priority is given to the id than the pneuma, because it titillates the flesh and makes no demands on the ego. The id belongs to what William James has called the once-born; the pneuma to those who are twice-born. We have three ways of knowing: One is by our senses, such as the clasp of a hand. The second is by abstract ideas and scientific training, such as the science of physics. Over and above both feeling and intellect, there is another kind of knowledge, such as that which a husband and wife attain after many years of married life — they have come to know one another by loving one another. This kind of knowledge the pneuma gives, only its love is more intense.

A new heart is created within us by a response to the pneuma. From the fleshy heart, there goes forth blood to the body and then a return flow to it. The heart understood psychologically also is understood as the center from which flows our mental and moral activity. From it comes all our character worth, and to it returns all our good merits; but the heart can also be the center of depravity that corrupts the whole circuit of life.

A boy in a family could not be induced to keep himself clean. He had dirty fingernails, hair hanging like a mop, clothes unpressed, dirty shoes. The parents begged, pleaded, coaxed, and even tried to bribe him into cleanliness. It did no good. But one day he appeared clean, brushed, and neat. He did not slam the door as he went out. What made the difference? He was in love with Suzie! This is the key to pneuma, the Spirit that reorients life; it is essentially love but not an earthly love.

As there are compulsive drinkers and compulsive addicts in the world, so there are compulsive lovers of humanity and compulsive lovers of Love in the pneuma world. We are no longer in the presence of demons and pink elephants, but of a Light that unfailingly allows us to follow footprints in the darkest forest of life.

I knew a man in London who told me that he had been an alcoholic for years; so enslaved was he that he would take off his shoes at the saloon door and sell them for a drink. This particular year he was seated on a bench at Hyde Park, musing about his miserable condition. Suddenly he felt a strong urge to reform his life. He professed ignorance as to where the resolution came from, but he said that it was not from himself. Following this inspiration was easy, but putting it into practice was difficult. He went into a church, and immediately there came over him an intense craving for drink. He ran to the rear of the church to escape, but he knelt down at the door. From that time on, the goal of his life was changed. He now spends his time caring for his fellow alcoholics in the same London dive where he lived for years. The day the inspiration seized him, he knew only one thing — it came not from himself. He had been hell-bent, and suddenly he was, after a struggle, on the heaven-bent road to inner happiness. The pneuma confronted him on the inside of his being, but it came from the outside. It was as if another Presence was in his life, acting like a radar bringing him to the port of peace.

Another example is given by the Russian novelist Tolstoy. His despairing nature drove him to the thought of suicide. Then, as he put it, something contrary to his mood seized him:

> I felt that something had broken within me on which my life had always rested, that I had nothing left to hold on to, and that morally my life had stopped. An invincible force impelled me to get rid of my existence, in one way or another.

Yet, whilst my intellect was working, something else in me was working too, and kept me from the deed — a consciousness of life, as I may call it, which was like a force that obliged my mind to fix itself on another direction, and draw me out of my situation of despair.

During the whole course of this year, when I almost unceasingly kept asking myself how to end the business, whether by the rope or by the bullet, during all that time, alongside of all those movements of my ideas and observations, my heart kept languishing with another pining emotion. I can call this by no other name than that of a thirst for God.

We have in our subconscious a mass of dead ideas, lifeless hopes, faded childhood memories, and lost faiths. We would like to get back to our innocence and joy, but they are cold and sepulchered. Then what was crucified by us suddenly rises from the dead; what was cold is now hot; what was crystal now becomes a living cell. What was on the periphery of life now becomes a center; what we ignored now is valued. And we know very well that this old building in which we lived, with its leaky plumbing and cracked walls, did not suddenly become a mansion without some builder from the outside. If my life is traveling in the direction of "confusion worse confounded," and all of a sudden changes its course, with new goals, then the Latin maxim applies: *Nihil movetur nisi per aliud movetur* ("Nothing is moved unless it is moved by another"). The new mental arrangement of ideas, the sudden thrust of some alien motor efficacy, demands a source outside of me and yet working inside me and principally through my subconsciousness.

The classic playboy of all antiquity was Augustine, who combined the greatness of the intellect with a sexual abandon that he justified by rationalization. One day the dissension between his sex life and his higher aspirations became so intense that he picked up St. Paul's Letter to the Romans; in it he read that not in wantonness, immorality, strife, and envy do we work out salvation. The words acted as a thunderbolt in Augustine's soul with his wasted young life. Changing the direction of his life after the impact of the pneuma, he cried out: "Too late, O Ancient Beauty, have I loved Thee!"

A spiritual knowledge under the pneuma is arrived at so quickly that the intellectual is left behind; one is not able to find a cause for the change in any previous thought. No one goes from the life of sin to holiness without some intervening cause that is sufficient to account for the change. What has taken place is nothing less than a divine-human encounter. A power enters into the subconsciousness that regenerates, changes direction, alters the moral character, making precious what was previously vile and vile what was previously precious.

No new faculties are created. They are just regenerated. What happens may be likened to putting a lamp inside the Japanese lantern. First it was nothing but a crisscross of crazy patterns. Once the light was put in it, there was a unification of color and line so that a pattern was revealed. The change may also be likened to a new kind of vision. We have the same eyes at night as we have in the day, but we cannot see at night because we lack the light of the sun. So a new light is given that enables us to see things that before we could not see.

Change never involves any violation of personality. There is no invasion like to what has been described as possession. But there is a *surrender* of self to Another. Looking back on the evil that one has done, one never sees it as a violation of the law, but rather as hurting someone we love. A new master center takes possession of personality and gives it what Frankl calls "a will to meaning." The whole life begins to be organized, not merely as a sum of parts but rather as a whole, very much the same as the melody that is heard very differently from the distinct notes on the paper.

Id requires analysis, because the mind is all mixed up. The pneuma synthesizes. To analyze the waters that pour into a sinking ship is not to save the ship; to plow by constantly looking back to see if the furrow is crooked may even make life more zigzag. Under probing, the true essence of life vanishes. Our physiological life demands harmony, the tiny cell choosing from its environment what it is able to assimilate; the psychological demands similar peace. A regulator, a kind of thermostat, is at the center of our organism, seeking to establish constants, such as temperature, blood pressure, and digestion. The automatic control is ever working to synthesize harmony and meaning.

So too there functions in the depths of our being another kind of regulator, or constant, summoning us back to order and to peace. Little warning lights begin to flicker as they do in the cockpit of a plane when anything is wrong, such as an unlocked door or an overheated motor. That is, organized sensitivity to the body becomes spiritual sensitivity in the conduct of our lives. A carpenter uses a gauge containing a colored liquid. He lays it on a board to see if it is level. Once he finds it off center, he begins to make the adjustment and correction. So too there is in us an adjuster that makes us rediscover inner peace and the true center, even in the midst of errors and excesses.

It has been proved medically that the power of healing wounds at a certain age increases when the temperature of the body is raised by four degrees. It is conceivable that the power of the pneuma, which increases the joy and the love in a person, may also accelerate the healing of the anxiety and chaos in the depths of being.

Now, what is this pneuma? Pneuma is the Spirit, the Spirit of God. As my body lives, thanks to my soul, so my soul begins really to live, thanks to the Spirit. Because this Spirit comes from outside us and is not either of our making or of our deserving, it is free or gratis or what is commonly called grace. The id draws to pleasure of the flesh; the pneuma to the joys of the spirit. It might be well to cut down on the temptations of the id and begin giving way to the temptations of the pneuma.

[FOOTPRINTS IN A DARKENED FOREST]

The Psychology
of Work

ERY FEW PEOPLE in this age do the kind of work they like to
do. Instead of choosing their jobs freely, they are forced by
economic necessity to work at tasks that fail to satisfy them.
Many of them say, "I ought to be doing something bigger," or "This job
of mine is only important because I get paid." Such an attitude lies at
the bottom of much unfinished and badly executed work. Those who
choose their work because it fulfills a purpose they approve are the only
ones who grow in stature by working. They alone can properly say, at
the end of it, "It is finished!"

This sense of vocation is sadly lacking nowadays. The blame should
not be placed on the complexity of our economic system, but on a
collapse of our spiritual values. Any work, viewed in its proper per-
spective, can be used to ennoble us; but a necessary prelude to seeing
this is to understand the philosophy of labor.

Every task we undertake has two aspects — our purpose, which
makes us think it worth doing, and the work itself, regarded apart from
its end-purpose. We play tennis to get exercise; but we play the game
as well as possible, just for the joy of doing the thing well. The man
or woman who argued that he or she could get as much exercise by
sloppy technique on the courts would have missed an understanding
of the second aspect of all activity: the accomplishment of the task

in accordance with its own standards of excellence. In the same way, someone working in an automobile factory may have, as his primary purpose, the earning of wages; but the purpose of the work itself is the excellent completion of the task. A worker should be aware of the second purpose at all times — as the artist is aware of the aim of beauty in his or her painting and the housekeeper is aware of the need for neatness when cleaning.

Today the first aspect of working has become paramount, and we tend to ignore the second, so that many workers lead half-lives in their laboring hours. They are like gardeners, ordered to grow cabbage to give them sauerkraut juice, but indifferent as to whether their plots are weeded properly or their cabbages are healthy vegetables. This is a mistaken attitude. God Himself worked when He made the world and then, viewing it, He called it "good."

Legitimate pride in doing work well relieves it of much of its drudgery. Some people, who have held to this craftsman's standard, get a thrill from any job they do. They know the satisfaction of "a job well done" whether they are engaged in caning a chair or cleaning a horse's stall or carving a statue for a cathedral. Their honor and their self-respect are heightened by the discipline of careful work. They have retained the old attitude of the Middle Ages, when work was a sacred event, a ceremony, a source of spiritual merit. Labor was not then undertaken merely for the sake of economic gain, but was chosen through an inner compulsion, through a desire to project the creative power of God through our own human effort.

No task should be undertaken in a spirit that ignores either of these two primary aspects of work. To link together the two things, the joy of making a table well with the purpose of making it at all, which is to earn a living, the following principles should be kept in mind:

(1) Work is a moral duty and not, as many imagine, a mere physical necessity. St. Paul said, *"Anyone unwilling to work should not eat"* (2 Thess 3:10). When work is seen as a moral duty, it is apparent that it not only contributes to the social good but also performs further services to the worker himself: It prevents the idleness from which

many evils can arise, and it also keeps one's body in subjection to the reasoned will.

(2) *"To work is to pray."* The well-regulated life does not defer prayer until work has been accomplished; it turns the work itself into a prayer. We accomplish this when we turn to God at the beginning and completion of each task and mentally offer it up for love of Him. Then, whether we are nursing a child or making carburetors, turning a lathe or running an elevator, the task is sanctified. No amount of piety in leisure hours can compensate for slipshod labor on the job. Any honest task, well done, can be turned into a prayer.

[WAY TO HAPPINESS]

When I resigned, I did not "retire." I *retreaded.* I took on another kind of work. I believe that we spend our last days very much the way that we lived. If we have lived with ease, taking our rest, never exerting ourselves, then we have a long dragging out of our days, like a slow leak. If we live intensely, I believe that somehow or other we can work up until the day God draws the line and says: "Now it is finished."

*   *   *

Retirement has many advantages. It becomes a time to remake one's soul, to interiorize, to meditate and begin a cram course for the final exam.

[TREASURE IN CLAY]

The Philosophy
of Pleasure

B
ECAUSE PLEASURE is the supreme goal of all egotistic living, it is fitting that we should know something of its laws. The very fury with which modern men and women seek pleasure is the strongest proof that they have not found it; for if the streets of our city were filled with clanging ambulances, and the hospitals were jammed to capacity, and nurses were running about madly, there would be a strong suspicion that health had not yet been found. Pleasure as a life goal is a mirage — no one reaches it. But it is possible to enjoy stable, refreshing pleasures, provided that one knows their laws.

The first law of pleasure is that it is like beauty: It is conditioned by contrast. A woman in white, if she has any esthetic sense, would rather stand before a black curtain than a white one. Similarly, every pleasure, to be enjoyed, must come as a sort of treat, as a surprise. The kind of pleasure that evokes laughter is an example: Incidents that are not funny on the street are hilarious in a church because of their contrast with the seriousness of the ritual — a man with his hat on the side of his head in the street does not provoke laughter, but a bishop with a miter on the side of his head does.

The condition of having a good time is that one shall not be always trying to have a good time. There is no fun in life, if everything is funny; there is no pleasure in shooting fireworks, if every day is the

Fourth of July. Many people miss pleasure because they seek nothing else, and so remove the first condition of enjoyment, which is contrast. In the liturgy of the Church, there is a constant contrast between joy and sacrifice, between fast and feast. Even during the seasons of Lent and Advent, when there is penance and pain, the Church inserts a Laetare and a Gaudete Sunday, on which we are called to rejoice. She does this, first of all, to remind people that penance is not perpetual; and, second, to prevent them from getting into a psychological rut.

The second law of pleasure is that no pleasure ever becomes our permanent possession until it has passed through a moment of pain. No one ever gets his second wind until he has used up his first wind; one never enjoys reading the Latin classics without having survived the tedium of grammar and declensions; to swim is a thrill, but only after the shock of the first cold plunge. Even the joys of eternity are conditioned by this law; for unless there is a Good Friday in life, there will never be an Easter Sunday; unless there is a crown of thorns, there will never be the halo of light; and unless there is a cross, there will never be the empty tomb. In our temporal concerns, too, the law prevails. In marriage, it is only after the first misunderstanding has been survived that a couple begins to discover the beautiful joy of being together.

The third law of pleasure is this: Every quest for pleasure is fundamentally a striving for the infinite. Every pleasure attracts us because we hope, by savoring it, to get a foretaste of something that will exceed it in intensity and joy. One bird, one star, one book, should be enough to fill our hunger, but it is not: We find no satisfaction in anything, because our appetites are formed for everything. Like a great vessel that is launched, we move insecurely in shallow waters, being made to skim the sea. To ask us to stop short of anything save the infinite is to nullify our nature; our greed for good is greater than the earth can gratify. All love of poetry is a cry, a moan, and a weeping; the more sublime and true it is, the deeper is its lament. If the joy of attaining something for which we longed ravishes the mind for an hour, it reverts, by evening, to the immensity of its still-unfulfilled desires.

The pursuit of pleasure is thus a token of our higher nature, a symptom of our loneliness in this world. Torn between what we have, which surfeits us, and the far-off Transcendent, which attracts us, all worldly persons stand in grave danger of self-hatred and despair until they find their true Infinite in God. As Pascal put it: "The knowledge of God without a perception of man's misery causes pride, and the knowledge of man's misery without a perception of God causes despair. Knowledge of Jesus Christ constitutes the middle course, because in Him we find both God and our own misery."

Until a person has discovered the true Infinite, that person is invariably led from subjectivism — the setting up of his or her ego as the absolute — to hedonism — the philosophy of a life given solely to sensate pleasures. When a person starts with the assumption that his selfish wishes must be held supreme, that nothing beyond the ego is significant, then it follows that the only standards by which he will be able to judge the worth of any experience are its pleasurableness and its intensity. The more that person feels something, the truer and more admirable it will be. There is a fallacy, however, lurking behind the hedonist's assumption that the motivation of every action is pleasure, for if this were the case, no hedonist would be moving about today; they would have lain on the ground and refused to stir the first time they fell down and hurt themselves as a child. A baby with bruised shins does not get up and try, again, to toddle, out of a search for pleasure, but because his drive to develop human capacities overcomes his desire for the pleasure of lying supinely on the floor. Pleasure is actually a by-product of duty, and it evades direct pursuit. It is like the bloom on the cheek, as Aristotle has told us; the bloom is not something we try to develop but is the by-product of a healthy organism.

The proper attitude toward life is not one of pleasure seeking, but the cultivation of a divine sense of humor within our human limitations. And what is humor? It is said that one has a sense of humor if he can "see the point" and that he lacks a sense of humor if "he cannot see the point." But God has made the world in such a way that He is the point of everything we see. The material is meant to be a revelation of the spiritual; the human, a revelation of the Divine; and the fleeting experiences of our days, a revelation of Eternity. The universe, according to God's original plan, was made transparent, like a windowpane. Everything created was to tell something about God, for "by the visible things of the world is the Invisible God made manifest" (Rom 1:20).

Such was God's drama, of which man was to play the role of lord of creation. When the lines were given to the first man to speak, he made a botch of them. That slip that destroyed man's role in creation was sin; and sin is a disproportionate seriousness. Sin was the act by which man refused to see creatures for what they were — steppingstones to God, a means to an end — and began, instead, to clutch at them as ends in themselves. That is what sin is, still. As those who lose their sense of humor when they cannot see the point of a pun, so we lose our sense of humor in its entirety when we cease to see the point of the universe, which is that all things are revelations, symbols, reminders of God Who made them. To take things seriously as ends in themselves is to overrate them, to treat them with a solemnity that is not warranted....

*   *   *

It could all be summed up in these words: "Nothing in this world is to be taken seriously — nothing except the salvation of a soul. The world, and the things that are in it, will one day be folded up like an Arab's tent; you are not to love exclusively for this life...." And still, today, there are the two possible outlooks on the world: either that of the hedonist, who is solemn about this world, considering it the only one that he will ever have; or that of the divine sense of humor, which permits a person to "see through" this world to the other world that he will have hereafter. The Christian can be careless of personal life and property. A child who has only one ball, which cannot be replaced, will be wary of using it. There will be a seriousness characterizing his play. But if he is told that he will some day be given another ball that will never wear out, he can take the first ball more lightly, can enjoy it without hoarding it.

Only those people who believe in transcendent reality can pass through this life with a sure sense of humor. The atheist, the agnostic, the skeptic, the materialist — all these have to take themselves seriously; they have no spiritual vantage point on which they can stand, look down upon themselves, and see how laughable they are. There is nothing more ludicrous than pretentiousness, and unless self-knowledge comes to puncture it, the absurdity will grow. Yet, if our self-exaltation is deflated without a recognition of the mercy of God, Who can lift up the sinner, then it may beget despair: God is required for gaiety.

There is only one place in Sacred Scripture where God is said to laugh: "He who sits in the heavens laughs; the Lord has them in derision" (Ps 2:4). We become laughable through our incongruities and our affectations. A boy of twelve who shaves, a girl of nine who dresses up like her mother will provoke laughter because they are posing as being something they are not. So, when the materialists or atheists set themselves up as God, denying any dependence on a Creator, repudiating their need of a Savior to forgive their faults and sins, then they become so ridiculous as to provoke the laughter of God Himself. And the pride of the scoffer is the thing that makes him doubly ridiculous. Two people on ice can fall, but if one of them is wearing a silk hat, that person will look funnier than the one who is dressed humbly. Self-exaltation humiliated and dignity punctured amuse us — and they may even amuse God. . . .

If God matters enough to us, His thumbprints are what make the visible world precious to us. If He chooses to remove some particular created thing, it cannot matter very much — for He Himself remains. When Job lost everything he had, he still maintained his divine sense of humor as he said: "The Lord gives, the Lord takes away, praised be the Lord" (Job 1:21). St. Francis viewed the universe with the same lighthearted wisdom when he claimed the moon for his sister and the sun for his brother, felt a creaturely kinship with fire and wind and water, and then, as he died, saluted death as a "welcome brother." Most of us become very provoked at mosquitoes, but St. Rose of Lima chose them as her favorite pets; they never harmed her, and she used to bid them sing to her as she prayed.

[Lift Up Your Heart]

The Tenderness
and Power

PASCAL SAID there were two things that frightened him. One was his own heart; the other, the silence of the eternal spheres. Immanuel Kant, the German philosopher, held that the two things that awed him were the moral law within his breast and the starry firmament above. There has always been a tendency in literature to put these two together, and with a certain justice, for only a Power great enough to control the heavens could ever solace the individual heart.

The Hebrew psalmist was the forerunner of those who set in contrast the providence of God, which was powerful enough to control the collective planets of the universe, and yet careful enough not to neglect the burden that weighed on a single heart. "He heals the brokenhearted, and binds up their wounds. He determines the number of the stars; he gives to all of them their names" (Ps 147:3–4).

There is hardly any physician or psychiatrist or friend who, in the face of a broken heart, would immediately think of countless stars or, contemplating the starry encampment of night, would ever think of the loneliness of the human breast. These are the two extremes that only great minds ever fit into one thought, namely, the bleeding heart and the fiery stars.

We lose the sense of the hour in studying history, and we forget the rolling scroll of history in the problem of an hour. It is the nature, however, of divine Love to assure us that He Who takes care of the great universe is the only One to Whom we can trust our life. The sovereign balm for every wounded heart comes only from Him from Whose fingertips there tumbled planets and worlds. Many a person has felt helplessness and loneliness beneath the stars, and yet Scripture says that star-counting and heart-healing go together.

There is a tendency today to believe that because the universe is far greater than we suspected, God perhaps is less perfect than we believed. This is part of the bad logic of Americans who judge the value of everything by its size. The truer point of view is that the greater the universe, the more certain we are to have our fretful mind lifted up to the thought of God's eternal presence and power. Then, too, the fact that we unite the planets and the heart is proof that the sorrows of this life are not nearly as akin to earth as they are to heaven. Sadness of human hearts cannot be explained by any philosopher on this earth, but only by God Who is powerful enough to make the stars and Who holds the secret of healing in His Own Divine Heart.

One finds the concretion and personalization of this relationship between hearts and stars in the contemplation of the Infinite God Who assumed a human nature, and yet could be solicitous of one lost sheep, a woman taken in sin, a blind man, a thief, and a broken-hearted widow following the body of her only son. It is not just sympathy that we need, but the consciousness that we are in the strong hands of the Lord of all. God is not remote from the little life down here on earth. We may ask how God could miss us from the fold when He is shepherding all the heavenly hosts. The answer is that God can find no room for His pity and no response to His love, nothing to bend over and heal and bless, except in our hearts. He Who holds all the nations in the palm of His hand is, nevertheless, the God of "Abraham and Isaac and of Jacob."

How often we say that it is very often the busiest person who is willing to help an individual. This is nothing but a confirmation that He Who made the heavens and lived for humanity spoke His tenderest love when His audience was one listener. Everyone else is too weak to heal a broken heart. He alone can do it Who counts the stars.

[Guide to Contentment]

Understanding Others

THE GOOD SAMARITAN has stood for centuries as the supreme example of one who had compassion on a fellow human being. The word "compassion" means "to suffer with" the afflicted, the poor, the hungry, and the thirsty.

The new compassion that has crept into our courts and into our literature and drama is the compassion for the breakers of the law, for the thieves, the drug dealers, the murderers, the rapists. This false compassion for the criminal and the readiness to blame the law and the police has passed from the "sob-sisters" to black-robed justices who, fearful of restraining a liberty turned into license, pardon the mugger and ignore the mugged.

This miscarriage of justice is found also in the inability of the prosperous to understand the unfortunate. The woes of widows, mothers with delinquent children, and cancer patients are often beyond the comprehension of would-be sympathizers. They think that they have sounded all depths and therefore are in a position to judge the merits of the one who is in agony. They have merely skimmed the surface. They do not know what others suffer; neither do they understand God's plan in relationship to them. Looking from sunny homes on the dark abodes of misery, they cannot understand the sorrows they have never tasted. Always having had their wants satisfied, they do not know the meaning of hunger and thirst.

It is part of our fallen nature to despise the trouble we do not understand. Not having the power to drive into the mystery, we see it as a shallow thing. When the sufferers complain much, we are inclined to think that they are exaggerating or giving way to cowardly weakness, just as the rich are too often ready to regard the very poor as whining imposters. Anyone who has never felt the pangs of conscience looks with contempt upon the penitent's tears. The Pharisees were very un-merciful to sinners, but a great sinner like Augustine could understand them well. When one is looking for counsel, it is always well to seek out those who themselves have suffered. There is much more wisdom acquired from patiently bearing suffering than there is from books. No one is ever consoled by having a moral theology flung at their head. Perhaps the reason why Peter and not John was chosen as the head of the Church was because he fell and, therefore, understood human weakness.

Suffering may be sent to us because we have been too narrow and selfish in our view of it, and also to prepare us for our work in helping others in trouble. The widow can sympathize with the widow; the poor show most kindness to the poor. The experience of the prostration of a great illness enables a person to understand and help sick people. Sorrow can thus become a talent to be used for the good of others by being invested in sympathy.

[GUIDE TO CONTENTMENT]

It Takes Three
to Make Love

L OVE IS VERY DIFFERENT from knowledge. When the mind is confronted with something above its level — for example, an abstract principle of metaphysics or mathematics — it breaks it down into examples so that it can understand it. The reason why many teachers fail in their profession is because they do not know how to bring down to a lower and concrete level the subject that they teach. Maybe they do not know the subject, for the test of knowing anything is the ability to give an example for it. Theses with footnotes, into which are thrown the knowledge that is not understood, are easier to write than a popularization of that same subject for a beginner. Some are thought to be learned when they are only confusing. The Lord spoke in terms of parables illustrating eternal verities, such as judgment of the good and bad, under the analogy of the separation of sheep and goats. If we understand anything, we can make it clear. If we do not understand it, we can never explain it.

But love acts just the opposite to knowledge. Love goes out to meet the demands of what is loved. The intellect pulls higher things *down* to its level; the will, which is the seat of love, lifts itself *up* to the level of the good that it loves. If one loves music, one meets the demands of music by submitting to its laws; if one wishes to win the love of a poet, one must cultivate some appreciation of poetry. Because love goes up to meet the beloved, it follows that the nobler the love, the nobler the character. We live on the plane of our loves....

* * *

Love exists not in isolation or suspension; it craves involvement with others because love is essentially a relation. Love of self becomes the love of others, either for the sake of association or for the continuation of humankind.

These two loves of self and neighbor ought to go together, but they often pull in opposite directions. On the one hand, we cannot cling to ourselves and love ourselves apart from all others, because the person who is absolutely alone is loveless. On the other hand, we cannot cling entirely to others, for though they offer an occasion of love, they also set limits to our love. They do this either because they are not absolutely lovable, or because they are really not worth clinging to at all. Loving self alone has many disadvantages: It forces us to dwell in quarters that are too cramped and squalid for comfort; it confronts self with a self that in some moments is not only unlovable but even intolerable; and it makes us want to get away from ourselves because we find we are not very deep. Probing into the depths of our ego to find peace is too often like plunging into a pool without water. After a while, our self-centeredness ends in self-disruption, as we discover we have no center at all. We cannot love ourselves properly unless we know why we are living.

Love is useless when alone, as it is in sleep or death. It is really possessed only by giving it to others. Love is a sign of our creatureliness, the strongest proof that we are not gods and have not all we need within ourselves. If we were God, we would have no need of loving anything else, for love would find its perfection within itself, as in God. We must love others because we are imperfect; it is the mark of our indigence, a reminder that we came from nothingness, and that of and by ourselves love is incomplete and sterile.

Yet in giving to others, we are often disappointed; some want to use us, others to possess us. The involvement does not come up to our expectations; the one whom we thought was a good angel turns out to be a fallen one. Some contacts with others are like boomerangs; they throw us back on ourselves poorer than when we left, and therefore embittered. Torn between the independence of their own ego and dependence on other egos, tossed between worship of self and worship of others, many hearts develop a restlessness and a fatigue that keep the rich busy running to psychoanalysts to have their anxiety explained away, and the poor having recourse to the cheaper charlatans of alcohol and sleeping tablets. It is interesting how a materialistic civilization describes the rich as suffering from an "anxiety neurosis," and the poor as being plain "nuts" or "crackpots." If no true solution of the tension between love of self and love of others is found, legitimate self-love degenerates into egotism, pride, skepticism, and arrogance, while love of others degenerates into lust, cruelty, and hatred of the spiritual. Cynics are disappointed egotists and revolutionists of violence are disgruntled altruists. Perverted self-love, when it became political, created individualism, or historical liberalism; perverted love of others, when it became political, created totalitarianism.

There is a solution to this problem of tension between love of the ego and love of the non-ego, or the independence of the ego and its dependence on other egos, but it is not to be found either in the ego or the non-ego. *The basic error of humankind has been to assume that only two are needed for love: you and me, or society and me, or humanity and me. Really it takes three: self, other selves, and God; you, and me, and God.* Love of self without love of God is selfishness; love of neighbor without love of God embraces only those who are pleasing to us, not those who are hateful. One cannot tie two sticks together without something outside the sticks; one cannot bind the nations of the world together except by the recognition of a Law and a Person outside the nations themselves. Duality in love is extinction through the exhaustion of self-giving. *Love is triune or it dies.* It requires three virtues, faith, hope, and charity, which intertwine, purify, and regenerate one another.

To *believe* in God is to throw ourselves in God's arms; to *hope* in God is to rest in His heart in patience amid trials and tribulations; to *love* God is to be with God through a participation of His divine nature through grace. If love did not have faith and trust, it would die; if love did not have hope, its sufferings would be torture, and love might seem loveless. Love of self, love of neighbor, and love of God go together and when separated fall apart.

[THREE TO GET MARRIED]

God does not love us because we are lovely or lovable; His love exists not on account of our character, but on account of His. Our highest experience is *responsive*, not initiative. And it is only because we are loved by Him that we are lovable.

[REJOICE!]

Love's Reaction to Loss

INASMUCH AS PSYCHONEUROSIS has become such a characteristic of our modern civilization, it is fitting that there be mirrored forth for the example of Christians the story of how one husband lived through its Golgothas and kept his faith in God.

Sophie-Charlotte Wittelsbach (1847–1897), at the age of nineteen, was betrothed to the king of Bavaria, who was already beginning to show signs of incipient insanity. The hopes of the young bride for an early marriage were wrecked, time and time again, as her prospective husband put off the marriage, and then, finally, told her that his only love in the world was for Wagnerian music. Her mind, somewhat shattered by this blow, found a temporary release when she met an exiled French Orléan, Ferdinand Philip, the duke of Alençon, whom she married. It was his first love, and his last love as he told her one day: "I have loved you with the most tender affections on this earth, for I love you with an eternal love because it is a Christian love."

This declaration of his love was made in the midst of a growing consciousness of her defects. Melancholia, which was one of the family traits, soon began to appear in her, manifesting itself in undue sensitiveness, impulsiveness, capriciousness, and morbidity. The young husband, with a prophetic intuition of her needs, began a passionate and pathetic fight to tear his wife away from the clutches of mental instability and her repeated relapses into disturbing psychoses and neuroses. The struggle that he faced was one that he confessed would require not only a husband much in love with his wife but also a guardian angel. He tried to introduce her to the realities of religion but without much success until he brought her to Rome for a visit, where he saw on an ancient tomb the inscription: "Sophronia may you live." Hundreds of times a day he recited the prayer for his wife, "Sophie may you live." Later on he changed it to an assertion: "Sophie, you *shall live.*"

After many years of suffering he said to his wife, in one of her rare moments of lucidity, "I have told you nothing in order not to trouble you, but I have been watching over you in silence. On the day of our marriage God gave you to me, body and soul. If, by chance, you happen to fall I would be the guilty one, for I answer for you and if I had remained not true it would have proven that I did not know how to preserve you." Despite her impossible conduct, her anti-religious outbursts, he never left her side except to visit their children in school.

Finally, when his wife had reached the age of thirty-six, through his patience and his prayers she emerged from her last and terrible crisis, transformed and transfigured. He joined the Third Order of St. Dominic and she joined the Third Order of St. Francis, and both united in works of charity. Many people began coming to her seeking her advice; the poor she visited on foot for many hours during the day and night; her former melancholia had given place to a joy that nothing could quench, and with that joy there came an amazing moral strength.

On the fourth of May in her fiftieth year she left her home to preside over a bazaar of charity that was then being held in Paris. The bazaar was a monstrous affair in a huge tent sheltering an array of tables and counters. The center of attraction was a recent invention, a motion-picture machine that was installed behind an arbor of flowers. Her husband had come to the bazaar in order to see his wife preside. Suddenly the motion-picture apparatus caught fire, and the two exits became jammed with escaping people. Because she presided, some people came to save her, but as she directed the women and children she said: "I shall go out last, save the others first." A Dominican nun who stood by her, seeing the flames coming closer, said: "My God, what an awful death." "Yes," smiled the duchess quietly, "but think of it, we shall see God in a few minutes."

Her husband, who tried to remain with her, was pushed by the crowd and left in a bedlam of smoke and fire and madness. The last that was seen of her was when she was kneeling by a young and fair girl, turning the latter's head toward her own bosom in order to hide from the young face the horrors of death. A few days later her husband, recovering consciousness in a hospital, was informed of his wife's death. His first words were: "Oh God, of course I know that I must not ask you why." Then a smile came over his lips, and resuming the prayer he learned at the ancient tomb in Rome, he now added a new invocation: the "Sophie may live," which later on became "Sophie, you shall live" now became: "Sophie, you live!"

[THREE TO GET MARRIED]

The more intensely we love, the less we think of a sacrifice involved to secure what we love.

[THOUGHTS FOR DAILY LIVING]

The Three Tensions of Love

THE PARADOX OF LOVE is that the human heart, which wants an eternal and ecstatic love, can also reach a moment when it has too much love and wishes to be loved no longer. Francis Thompson in a poem tells how he picked up a child to hold, and held him in his arms, and how the child cried and kicked to get down. On reflecting, he wondered if that is not the way some souls are before God. They are not ready to be loved by God.

Certainly some such moment comes in the human order when there is a tug of war between wanting love and not wanting it. What is this mysterious alchemy inside the human heart that makes it swing between a feeling that it is not loved enough and the feeling that it is loved too much? Torn between longing and satiety, between craving and disgust, between desire and satisfaction, the human heart queries: Why should I be this way? When satiety comes, the "thou" disappears, in the sense that it is no longer wanted. When longing reappears, the "thou" becomes a necessity. Loved too much, there is discontent; loved too little, there is an emptiness. . . .

* * *

If love remained only in the flesh and were like a bitter weed that would suffer no flowers to bloom except its own, love would be most miserable, for love then would only be a quest and not a communion. Love that is only a search or a quest is incomplete. All incompleteness ends in frustration. The difficulty all who are married must feel is the paradox of the romance and the marriage, the chase and the capture. Each has its joys, but never perfectly are they combined here below. The marriage ends the courtship; the courtship presupposes no marriage. The chase ends with the capture. How is this contradiction met? There is only one way that will not sear the soul, and that is to see that both the marriage and the courtship are incomplete. The courtship was really a quest for the infinite, and a search for an unending, ecstatic, eternal love, while the marriage was the possession of a finite and fragmentary love, however blissful might be its moments. The search was for the garden; it ended in eating the apple. The quest was for the melody; the discovery was only a note.

At this point Christianity suggests: Do not think that life is a snare or an illusion. It would be that *only* if there were no Infinite to satisfy your yearnings. Rather, husband and wife should say: "We both want a love that will never die and will have no moments of hate or satiety. That love lies beyond both of us; let us, therefore, use our marital love one for another to bring us to that perfect, blissful love, which is God." At that point, love ceases to be a disillusionment and begins to be a sacrament, a material, carnal channel toward the spiritual and the divine. Husband and wife then come to see that human love is a spark from the great flame of eternity; that the happiness that comes from the unity of two in one flesh is a prelude to that greater communion of two in one spirit. In this way, marriage becomes a tuning fork to the song of the angels, or a river that runs to the sea.

The couple then sees that there is an answer to the elusive mystery of love, and that somewhere there is a reconciliation of the quest and the goal, and that is in final union with God, where the chase and capture, the romance and the marriage, fuse into one. For since God is boundless eternal Love, it will take an ecstatic eternal chase to sound its depths. At one and the same eternal moment, there is a limitless receptivity and a boundless gift. Thus does *eros* climb to *agape*, and both move on to that greatest revelation ever given to the world: *God is love.*

[THREE TO GET MARRIED]

Love has two terms: He Who Loves and He Who is loved. In love the two are reciprocal. I love and I am loved. Between me and the one I love there is a bond. It is not my love; it is not his love; it is our love; the mysterious resultant of two affections, a bond that enchains, and an embrace wherein two hearts leap with but a single joy.

[THE DIVINE ROMANCE]

Love Is a Messenger

THE CURVE OF LOVE was meant to be an ascension, for love is a messenger. A messenger brings an envelope or a package that is visible and material; but inside the envelope is something invisible and immaterial. Life is like that, and love is like that. A handshake is a messenger. It is much more than the clasping of two hands, for if we clasp our own hands, we would never say that it was a handshake. The material element, or that which is seen, is the grasping of the hand; the invisible element is the communication of welcome and friendship. A word has something audible or material about it, for it causes vibrations in the air; but there is something invisible about it, namely, the meaning that only a mind can perceive. A dog hears the sound of a word just as well as a human being, but the dog does not grasp the meaning of the sound. An engagement ring is a messenger that tells the story of a pledge of love. Beyond the material value of the ring is the invisible and unseen assurance of being loved; that is why the ring is placed on the finger that the ancients believed had a vein that led directly to the heart. The veil that a woman wears on her wedding day is also a messenger. Even among the Moslems, neither to make the woman ineffective, nor to hide her personality; rather, the veil is a symbol of the invisible, a token that all has not been disclosed, a reminder that there are mysteries not yet sounded and treasures not yet discovered.

Love was meant to be also a sign, a symbol, a messenger, a telltale of the Divine. The material element in it is the love shown to one another by husband and wife. The invisible spiritual element is the fact that all love comes from God. Love is a messenger from God saying that every human affection and every ecstasy of love are sparks from the great flame of love that is God. Love is very much like sunlight, which in prehistoric time bathed the trees of the forest. Later on, the trees sank into the earth and finally were dug up as coal. When the coal burns, it returns again the debt of light and heat that it took from the sun. So the human heart receives its capacity and its desire for love from God as the trees receive sunlight; later on, in union with another heart, love burns and returns again to God the love that came from Him.

A person who turns on an electric switch in the house may live under the illusion that he himself has caused the light that is in the room, but actually at a great distance is a dynamo that supplies the electricity. We do not create, but merely utilize, the power. When one person falls in love with another, he or she is merely turning on the switch that releases the tremendous reservoir of love that has its source in the Infinite. One heart, one flower, one sunset, ought to be enough to satisfy the human heart if it were made only for this world; but the constant search for the "more" is an indication that we were made for something greater than any love we find on this earth. Only the universal can give us contentment, but here below we find only the particular. We want the garden, and we get green apples.

Here are three reasons why love is the messenger of the Infinite. First, no human heart is satisfied totally and completely with any love that it finds on earth. From the cradle to the grave, we are in search of an ecstasy that has no satiety and a love that has no ending. The search for love begins as the infant presses himself to his mother's breast; later on, the child goes to his mother to have his play wounds bound; in adolescence, youth seeks out a companion, young, like himself, to whom he can unpack his heart with words. Then he seals his love in marriage. And so the quest for love continues from the cradle to the grave.

But love is not found here in all its fullness — broken hearts, ruined homes, disillusionment, divorce, all prove that the totality of love has not yet been discovered. Even when love does remain fine and noble and pure, a day must come when the last cake is crumbled at life's great feast, the last embrace is passed from friend to friend, and there is nothing perfect that ends.

We must not be cynical about the love that is given on earth. Searching for the source of love is very much like looking for the source of light on the stage. The source is not to be found under the scenery, for there light is mixed with darkness; it is not to be found under the cameras, for there light is mingled with shadow. Reason tells us that, if we are to find the source of the light in this theater, we must go out to a light that is not mingled with its shadow, namely, the pure light. Reason also tells us that, if we are to find the source of the love that is in this world, we must go out to a love that is not mingled with its shadow, hate or death, but must go out to Pure Love, and that is the definition of God. Every human heart that enjoys a rapture of love is receiving a fraction of that love and will never be happy until it possesses the ecstasy of the whole.

We would never want the infinite ecstasy if we were not made for it. We would never have eyes unless there was light; we would never have ears unless there were sounds; we would never have stomachs unless there was food; and we would never have the heart craving enduring love unless there was a God to supply it. Love exists in ideal before it exists in fact. That is why many hearts carry around a blueprint of the one that they love; when they see that love realized, it comes to them as the fulfillment of a dream....

A second reason why love is a messenger revealing God's love is that all lovers speak of "our love." They imply that love is something more than the sum of their love one for another. They suggest that there is some power and force outside of them that pulls them together. They often speak of a power that is greater than their own. Two pencils cannot be tied together except by a string outside of the pencils themselves. Two persons cannot be tied together unless they are bathed in the great ocean of love that comes from God. Fish have communion one with the other because they bathe in the depths of the ocean. As our eyes live in the great environment of light, so too all the human hearts in the world bathe in a much more mysterious way in that great ocean of love that is infinite.

A third reason why love is a messenger is this: *Every man and woman in love promise one another something that only God can give.* Why is love so rich in promise and so miserly in fulfillment? A promise is in the future and therefore is infinite in possibilities; the present, however, is a finite realization. When, therefore, a man and woman promise one another infinite perfect happiness, they are actually promising something that they cannot deliver; they are selling one another the Brooklyn Bridge. There is much unhappiness ahead when the flickering, smoldering wax promises to give the light that belongs to the sun. The ocean is jealous of its depths and will revenge itself on the little stream that promises the forest a fountain.

[LOVE, MARRIAGE AND CHILDREN]

Certain things that we have in us, once they are given out, are never meant to be taken back. One is the air we breathe; if we take that air back upon ourselves, it poisons us. Love is another. When love is breathed out to another human heart, it is never meant to be taken back. If it is taken back, it suffocates and poisons us.

[LIFE IS WORTH LIVING]

Altruism: The Evolution of Love

OUR WORLD has been too much impressed by both Darwin and Marx; it is not correct to believe that life is to be explained in terms of the Darwinian struggle for existence and the Marxist terms of class conflict. Tennyson was not wholly right in describing "nature red in tooth and claw," for the truth is that most teeth and claws are not red but green with chlorophyll and life.

A more scientific view of nature sees it, not only as a scene of struggle, but also as a stage for altruism. Nature is full of cooperation, affection, harmony, benevolence, chivalry, generosity, in which the chord of self is struck in order to make music for others. Take a survey of nature and it will be discovered that it is unconsciously preparing for love in man.

Consider first the sun. It is over 92 million miles away from this earth, yet it is burning itself away at the rate of 365,000 tons a day in order to light this world. Sunbeams are shining ghosts of defunct matter; electrons and protons are falling into each other's arms and vanishing into radiation for the sake of the earth.

Volcanoes, in their turn, after the crashing of suns and planets, are less bent on the destruction of life than on being a nursery for it. The water that is on the earth was formed from the condensed steam of primitive volcanoes. Minerals dissolved from these hot streams as they hissed from the crater's mouth and drooling lips. Rolling down the sides of the volcanoes, they became streams and rivers and oceans. The chemicals in these waters prepared for blood. Nature did not draw blood from stone, but from red-hot lava. In a certain sense, the volcanoes suffered a veritable hemorrhage of blood, for the primitive sea contained all of the mineral salts, albuminous substances, and oxygen that the first sea creatures needed. Mammalian blood has ingeniously maintained the original temperature of 99 to 100°F, and is still a solution of 8 parts in 1,000 of some twenty or more chemical salts. The Greeks used to say that all life came from water. Maybe they were not so wrong, for Our Blessed Lord certainly said that divine Life came from water.

Plants, too, tell us that life must live not only for itself, but also for others. The trunk and the branches are for self, but the blossoms are for a generation yet unborn. The lesson of altruism is hidden in every blossom. The blossom is one of the first blushes of motherhood that nature knows. So much is the noble tree bound up with altruism that ofttimes reproduction is hastened by wounding it, as if to remind us that sacrifice and surrender are the conditions of a new and richer Life. When an apple falls to the ground, the outer pulp decays and rots, but inside of it are seeds that are the promise of immortality. This may be a dim suggestion that when we shuffle off our mortal coil, there is hidden within the outer pulp, a soul that is the seed of true immortality.

In pre-Bolshevik days, a distinguished Russian scientist by the name of Timiriazeff planted a willow tree weighing 5 pounds in 200 pounds of soil. After five years he took out the tree, weighed it, and found that it had increased to 169 pounds 3 ounces. Carefully weighing the soil, he discovered that there had been a loss of only 2 ounces. The increase of over 164 pounds in the weight of the willow was due to its nourishment and communion with the great, invisible forces of light and heat. Lower nature is not the sole explanation of growth of the tree. This is a dim reminder that humanity's true growth is through communion with the spiritual forces that issue from the heart of God.

One of the lowest forms of animal life is the amoeba; while it has to struggle for its own existence, it also suggests thoughtfulness for others. The amoeba has only one cell; yet there comes a moment in its life when it has to decide whether or not it will live only for itself, or sacrifice a part of itself in order that another life may live. As it reproduces itself by fission, or splitting, there is a physical forecast of something noble in the universe. Unconsciously it perceives that it must either reproduce itself or die; it saves the species by sacrifice, and thus is a kind of Old Testament preparation for the higher love in human nature. All through nature, those communities that include the greatest number of sympathetic members flourish best; those that manifest the greatest mutual aid have the best chance of survival. Nature is never purposefully cruel.

Love begins to be conscious in the human being. In nature, altruism is necessary; within humanity, it is free. It is the possibility of "no" that gives so much charm to "yes."

There are five ways in which a human can love others. The first is *utilitarian* love, which is directed to another because he is useful to us. "He can get it at wholesale." "He knows where to buy minks at a discount." The difficulty with this kind of love is that when the advantage is lost, the friendship no longer endures.

The second kind of love is *romantic* love. This is the kind of affection we bear to another because of the pleasure that the other person gives us. The "I" is projected into the "thou," and though the "thou" is pretended to be loved, actually what is loved is the "I" that is in it. One of the reasons why many modern marriages do not endure is that people do not marry a person: They marry an experience. They fall in love with an ecstasy or a thrill, loving the cake only as long as it has frosting on it.

The third kind of love that one can have for another is *democratic* love, which is based upon equality under the law. Others are respected because they are fellow citizens; or their liberties are recognized, in order that ours, in their turn, may be recognized. The reason for contributing to the good of others is the expectation of a return good.

Democratic love, however, functions only up to a certain point; it is often subtracted in competition, or else invalidated on the assumption that the other person is "not worthy" of our affection. Democratic love is often under a great strain during a political campaign as candidates call one another "cheap politicians." There is no such thing in all the world as a "*cheap* politician."

The fourth kind of love, which has given much inspiration to poetry, is *humanitarian* love, which is love for humanity in general. One of the defects of this type of love is that it is love in the abstract, rather than in the concrete; it is love at a distance, rather than an immediate service. It is a historical fact that those who have most proclaimed their love of humanity have found it very difficult to love certain human beings. Humanity is like a composite photograph: It is nobody in particular. Dostoevsky makes one of his better characters describe the insufficiency of this type of love: "I love humanity but I wonder at myself, because the more I love humanity in general, the less I love man in particular. In my dreams I have come to make enthusiastic schemes for the service of humanity, and perhaps I might actually have faced a crucifixion had it been suddenly necessary, and yet, I am incapable of living in the same room with anyone two days together, as I know by experience. As soon as anyone is near me, his personality disturbs my self-complacency and restricts my freedom. In twenty-four hours I begin to hate the best of men; one because he is too long over his dinner; one because he has a cold and keeps blowing his nose. I become hostile to people the moment they come close to me, but it has always happened that the more I detest men individually, the more ardent becomes my love of humanity."

Surpassing these four kinds of love is *Christian* love summarized in the words of Our Savior: "A new commandment I give unto you that you love one another as I have loved you" (Jn 13:34). What is new about this commandment? Did not the Old Law say, "Love one another"? Have not all ethical teachers through the centuries pleaded for altruism? What is new about it? Two things are new. First, the way Our Lord loved us, that is, to a point of self-sacrifice; second, it is new because it is a commandment. By making it a commandment, Our Divine Lord made a distinction between liking and loving. Liking is in the emotions, in the temperament, in the glands, in feelings, and over these we have little or no control. Loving, however, is in the will and, therefore, is subject to command. There are certain things we do not like, and we cannot help not liking them. For example, some do not like fat people in tweeds; others cannot bear olives at the bottom of Martini glasses. I do not like chicken. Instinctive reactions in us we cannot completely control, but by putting love in the will, we can control it, and even extend it to those whom we do not like. Love, then, is not a gush but a virtue; not a spasmodic enthusiasm, but an abiding relationship of service, affection, and sacrifice.

The commandment is new, not only because it is in the will, but also because the model of such love is God Himself: "As I have loved you." He loved us when as yet we were sinners. When anyone does us wrong, we say, "You lost my love; change, and then I will love you." Our Blessed Lord, on the contrary, says, "Love someone, and then he will change. Let your love be the creation of his betterment." It was the love that He gave Peter the night that Peter denied Him that made Peter change. Tradition has it that Peter went out and wept so much that he created furrows in his checks because he had hurt someone whom he loved.

Our Blessed Lord gave the test of love when He said, "Love your enemies." We are not to expect anything in return, but to go on loving even in the midst of hostility and persecution. Love is disinterested when it continues despite hate. By making the love of neighbor an affair of the will, and not a matter of feeling, Our Savior took love out of the narrow circle of self, exiled it from the "I" castle, and set it fully on the side of the other person. He urged that we so efface self that we care for other persons for *their* sake alone and not for any ulterior purpose. We cross over the chasm and become the other person's possession.

One way of knowing whether our love is totally disinterested is to compare it with the love we have for those who are dead. Here is absolutely no possibility of requital, return of friendship, pleasure, or utility. When love persists even without a return of love, then is the affection pure. Nature bids us be mindful of others; Christ bids us to put love where we do not find it, and thus will we find everyone lovable.

[LOVE, MARRIAGE AND CHILDREN]

Love is not just an affirmation, but a negation; it implies sacrifice — a surrender of our will, of our selfish interests, for the good of the other. It looks not to the lover's pleasure, but to the happiness of the beloved.

[GOD AND WAR]

Are You Happy?

IF YOU SAW HORDES of peoples tramping the fields, with axes in their hands and pans strapped to their shoulders, you would conclude that those people had not found all the gold they wanted. If you saw armies of nurses and doctors riding ambulances, or carrying cots, you would conclude that health had not been found. When you see people crowding into theaters, charging cocktail bars, seeking new thrills in a spirit of restlessness, you would conclude that they have not yet found pleasure, otherwise they would not be looking for it.

The very fact that you can conceive of greater happiness than you possess now is a proof that you are not happy. If you were perfect, you would be happy. There is no doubt that at one time or other in your life you attained that which you believed would make you happy, but when you got what you wanted, were you happy?

Do you remember when you were a child, how ardently you looked forward to Christmas? How happy you thought you would be, with your fill of cakes, your hands glutted with toys, and your eyes dancing with the lights on the tree!

Christmas came, and after you had eaten your fill, blown out the last Christmas light, and played till your toys no longer amused, you climbed into your bed, and said in your own little heart of hearts that somehow or other it did not quite come up to your expectations. Have you not lived that experience over a thousand times since?

You looked forward to the joys of travel, but when weary feet carried you home, you admitted that the two happiest days were the day you left home and the day you got back. Perhaps you thought it was marriage that would bring you perfect happiness. Even though it did bring a measure of happiness, you admit that you now take your companion's love for granted. . . .

Perhaps it was wealth you wanted. You got it, and now you are afraid of losing it. "A golden bit does not make the better horse." Our happiness truly does not consist in the abundance of the things we possess. Maybe it was a desire to be well-known that you craved. You did become well-known only to find that reputation is like a ball: As soon as it starts rolling, people begin to kick it around.

The fact is you want to be perfectly happy, but you are not. Your life has been a series of disappointments, shocks, and disillusionments. How have you reacted to your disappointments? Either you became cynical or else you became religious.

If you became cynical, you decided that, since life is a snare and a delusion, you ought to get as much fun out of it as possible. In such a case you clutched at every titillation and excitement your senses afforded, making your life an incessant quest of what you called a "good time." Or else you reacted to disappointments by becoming religious and saying: "If I want happiness, I must have been made for it. If I am disappointed here, it must be that I am seeking happiness in the wrong places. I must look for it somewhere else, namely, in God."

Here is a fallacy to the first reaction: believing that the purpose of life is to get as much pleasure out of it as possible. This would be the right attitude if you were just an animal. But you have a soul as well as a body. Hence, there are joys in life as well as pleasures.

There is a world of difference between the two. Pleasure is of the body; joy is of the mind and heart. Lobster Newburg gives pleasure to certain people, but not even the most avid lobster fans would ever say that it made them joyful. You can quickly become tired of pleasures, but you never tire of joys. Children think they never could get too much ice cream, but they soon discover there is just not enough "child" to fill.

A pleasure can be increased to a point where it ceases to be a pleasure; it may even begin to be a pain if carried beyond a certain point; for example, tickling or drinking. But the joy of a good conscience, or the discovery of a truth, never turns to pain.

Humans can become dizzy from the pleasure of drink, but no one ever became dizzy from the joy of prayer. A light can be so bright it will blind the eye, but no idea was ever so bright as to kill the mind; in fact, the stronger and clearer the idea, the greater its joy. If, therefore, you live for pleasure, you are missing the joys of life.

Furthermore, have you noticed that as your desire for pleasure increased, the satisfaction from the pleasure decreased? The drug addict, to have an equal pleasure, must increase his dose. Do you think a philosophy of life is right that is based on the law of diminishing returns? If you were made for pleasure, why should your capacity for pleasure diminish with the years instead of increase?

Then, too, have you observed that your pleasures were always greater in anticipation than in realization? With the joys of the spirit, it is just the contrary. The cross, for example, is unattractive in prospect, but is sweet in possession. To Judas, the prospect of thirty pieces of silver was attractive, but he brought back his thirty pieces of silver. He got what he wanted and it filled him with disgust.

If your philosophy is always to have a good time, you have long ago discovered that you never really have a good time, for you are always in pursuit of happiness without ever capturing it. By a twist of nature, you make your happiness consist in the quest for happiness, rather than in happiness itself, just as so many modern professors much prefer to seek the truth than to find it. You thus become most hungry where you are most satisfied.

When the first thrill of ownership is gone, and your possessions begin to cloy, your sole happiness now is in pursuit of more possessions. You turn the pages of life, but you never read the book.

That is why those who live only for pleasure become cynical in middle age. A cynic has been defined as one who knows the price of everything and the value of nothing. You blame things, rather than self. If you are married, you say: "If I had another husband, or another wife, I could be happy." Or you say, "If I had another job...,"; or, "If I visited another night-club...,"; or, "If I were in another city, I would be happy." In every instance, you make happiness *extrinsic* to yourself. No wonder *you* are never happy. You are chasing mirages until death overtakes you.

Never will you find the happiness you crave, because your desires conflict. Despite the advertisements, "Eat and dance," you cannot do both at the same time. There is an exclusiveness about certain pleasures; they cannot be enjoyed in company with others. You cannot enjoy a good book and a football game at the same time. You cannot make a club sandwich of the pleasures of swimming and skiing. Even the best of pleasures, such as the enjoyment of good music or literature, cannot go on indefinitely, for human resources are incapable of enjoying them without relaxation. There may be no limit to our returning to them, but there is a limit to our staying with them.

Your whole life is disordered and miserable if it is based on the principle of always having a good time, simply because happiness is a by-product, not a goal; it is the bridesmaid, not the bride; it flows from something else. You do not eat to be happy; you are happy because you eat. Hence, until you find out what your purpose in life is, you will never really have a good time.

Time is the greatest obstacle in the world to happiness, not only because it makes you take pleasures successively, but also because you are never really happy until you are unconscious of the passing of time! The more you look at the clock, the less happy you are. The more you enjoy yourself, the less conscious you are of the passing of time. You say, "Time passed like everything." Maybe, therefore, your happiness has something to do with the eternal. You can find happinesses in time, but what you want is happiness that is timeless.

The other reaction to disappointment is much more reasonable. It begins by asking: "Why am I disappointed?" and then, "How can I avoid it?"

Why are you disappointed? Because of the tremendous disproportion between your desires and your realizations. Your soul has a certain infinity about it because it is spiritual; but your body and the world about you are material, limited, "cabined, cribbed, confined." You can imagine a mountain of gold, but you will never see one. You can imagine a castle of 100,000 rooms, one room studded with diamonds, another with emeralds, another with pearls, but you will never see such a castle.

In like manner, you look forward to some earthly pleasure, or position, or state of life, but, once you attain it, you begin to feel the tremendous disproportion between the ideal you imagined and the reality you possess. Disappointment follows. Every earthly ideal is lost by being possessed. The more material your ideal, the greater the disappointment; the more spiritual it is, the less the disillusionment. That is why those who dedicate themselves to spiritual interests, such as the pursuit of truth, never wake up in the morning with a dark brown taste in their mouths, or a feeling that they are run down at the heels.

Having discovered why you are disappointed, namely, because of the distance between an ideal conceived in the mind and its actualization in flesh or matter, you do not become a cynic. Rather, you take the next step of trying to avoid disappointments entirely. There is nothing abnormal about your wanting to live, not for two more years, but always; there is nothing odd about your desiring truth, not the truths of economics to the exclusion of history, but all truth; there is nothing inhuman about your craving for love, not until death do you part, not until satiety sets in or betrayal kills, but always.

Certainly you would never want this perfect Life, perfect Truth, and perfect Love unless it existed. The very fact that you enjoy their fractions means there must be a whole. You would never know their arc unless there were a circumference; you would never walk in their shadows unless there were light.

Would a duck have the instinct to swim if there were no water? Would a baby cry for nourishment if there were no such thing as food? Would there be an eye unless there were beauty to see? Would there be ears unless there were harmonies to hear? And would there be in you a craving for unending life, perfect truth, and ecstatic love unless perfect Life and Truth and Love existed?

In other words, you were made for God. Nothing short of the Infinite satisfies you, and to ask you to be satisfied with less would be to destroy your nature.

Your mind, it would seem, should be satisfied to know one leaf, one tree, or one rose; but it never cries: "Enough." Your craving for love is never satisfied. All the poetry of love is a cry, a moan and a weeping. The more pure it is, the more it pleads; the more it is lifted above the earth, the more it laments. If a cry of joy and ravishment interrupts this plea, it is only for a moment, as it falls back again into the immensity of desires. You are right in filling the earth with the chant of your heart's great longing, for you were made for love.

No earthly beauty satiates you either for, when beauty fades from your eyes, you revive it, more beautiful still in your imagination. Even when you go blind, your mind still presents its image before you, without fault, without limits, and without shadow. Where is that ideal beauty of which you dream? Is not all earthly loveliness the shadow of something infinitely greater? No wonder Virgil wished to burn his *Aeneid,* and Phidias cast his chisel into the fire. The closer they got to beauty, the more it seemed to fly from them, for ideal beauty is not in time but in the Infinite.

Despite your every straining to find your ideals satisfied here below, the Infinite torments you. The splendor of an evening sun as it sets like a "host in the golden monstrance of the west," the breath of a spring wind, the divine purity in the face of a Madonna, all fill you with a nostalgia, a yearning, for something more beautiful still.

With your feet on earth, you dream of heaven; creature of time, you despise it; flower of a day, you seek to eternalize yourself. Why do you want Life, Truth, Beauty, Goodness, and Justice, unless you were made for them? Whence come they? Where is the source of light in the city street at noon? Not under autos, buses, nor the feet of trampling throngs, because there light is mingled with darkness. If you are to find the source of light, you must go out to something that has no admixture of darkness or shadow, namely, to pure light, which is the sun.

In like manner, if you are to find the source of Life, Truth, and Love, you must go out to...something that is Pure Life, Pure Truth, Pure Love, and that is God. And the reason you have been disappointed is that you have not yet found God!...

*   *   *

It is God for Whom we are looking. Your unhappiness is not due to your want of a fortune, or high position, or fame, or sufficient vitamins; it is due not to a want of something *outside* you, but to a want of something *inside* you. You cannot satisfy a soul with husks! If the sun could speak, it would say that it was happy when shining; if a pencil could speak, it would say that it was happy when writing — for these were the purposes for which they were made. You were made for perfect happiness. That is your purpose. No wonder everything short of God disappoints you.

But have you noticed that when you realize you were made for perfect happiness, how much less disappointing the pleasures of earth become? You cease expecting to get silk purses out of sows' ears. Once you realize that God is your end, you are not disappointed, for you put no more hope in things than they can bear. You cease looking for first-rate joys where only tenth-rate pleasures are to be found.

You begin to see that friendship, the joys of marriage, the thrill of possession, the sunset and the evening star, masterpieces of art and music, the gold and silver of earth, the industries and the comforts of life, are all the gifts of God. He dropped them on the roadway of life, to remind you that if these are so beautiful, then what must be Beauty!

Unfortunately, many become so enamored of the gifts the great Giver of Life has dropped on the roadway of life that they build their cities around the gift, and forget the giver; and when the gifts, out of loyalty to their Maker, fail to give these people perfect happiness, they rebel against God and become cynical and disillusioned.

Change your entire point of view! Life is not a mockery. Disappointments are merely markers on the road of life, saying: "Perfect happiness is not here." Every disillusionment, every blasted earthly hope, every frustrated human desire, points to God. You can come to God not only by being good, but, if you only knew it, by a succession of disgusts.

The very sense of loss you feel in this world is in itself a proof that once you were possessed, and possessed by God. Though your *passions* may have been satisfied, *you* were never satisfied, because while your passions can find satisfaction in this world, you cannot. If at the present time vices have left you, do not think that you have left your vices.

Start with your own insufficiency and begin a search for perfection. Begin with your own emptiness and seek Him who can fill it. But you must be aware of your loneliness and want and disappointment before you can want Him to supply it. "Search, and you will find" (Mt 7:7).

Look at your heart! It tells the story of why you were made. It is not perfect in shape and contour, like a Valentine heart. There seems to be a small piece missing out of the side of every human heart. That may be to symbolize a piece that was torn out of the Heart of Christ, which embraced all humanity on the Cross.

I think the real meaning is, that when God made your human heart, He found it so good and so lovable that He kept a small sample of it in heaven. He sent the rest of it into this world to enjoy His gifts, and to use them as stepping-stones back to Him, but to be ever mindful that you can never love anything in this world with your whole heart because you have not a whole heart with which to love. In order to love anyone with your whole heart, in order to be really peaceful, in order to be really whole-hearted, you must go back again to God to recover the piece He has been keeping for you from all eternity.

[PREFACE TO RELIGION]

The Continuation of
the Incarnation

THERE ARE TWO KINDS OF TRUTH: outer and inner. An *outer* truth is one we master; e.g., the distance of the sun from the earth. An *inner* truth is one that masters us; e.g., God is merciful to the penitent. Outer truths of physics and chemistry come to us without desire, sorrow, pity, or emotion. Inner truths carry some emotion with them and influence behavior; one cannot be indifferent to them. They are connected with purity of motive.

St. Thomas notes how differently a moral theologian understands chastity when he lectures about it than a person who has lived chastely for years. The latter has endured it and existentialized it as an inner truth. Some read the Bible as a lawyer might read a will, studying all the technical loopholes and exactness of phrase. How differently the heir reads the will. In like manner, the teacher who practices what he or she preaches will influence students more than the mouthers of textbooks. The listeners to unvirtuous teachers may well say: "I cannot hear what you say because I see the way that you live."

The correlation between the way I preach and the way I live is intimate. The Levites and priests who passed by the wounded man were probably on their way to the temple for liturgy or else to preach on "Love." Credibility and behavior are twins. Only those who practice their convictions are believable. Otherwise they are like announcers urging the viewer to buy a Chevrolet while they drive a Plymouth. There was some truth in the cry of Bonhoeffer during the Nazi days: "Only he who cries out in defense of the Jews dare permit himself to sing Gregorian!"

The preacher who bores others in the pulpit is a bore before he gets into it. He is not in love. He is not on fire with Christ. He is a burned-out cinder floating in the immensity of catchwords. "For words that the mouth utters come from the overflowing of the heart" (Lk 6:45). Some other source than Christ is behind the sociological platitudes, moral chestnuts, and political bromides of the preacher.

Many of those in the pews today have sheepskins from colleges, and they are impatient of truthless priests who try to pull the wool over their eyes. The "lips of the priest shall contain knowledge"; priests must understand different approaches to their audience — for example, souls are not going to God today through the *order* in the universe; they are going to God through the *disorder* in their own souls. Hence, attention to the anxieties, fears, remorses and pains in the human heart. Psychological axioms are not deep enough to touch torn souls.

[THOSE MYSTERIOUS PRIESTS]

Selfishness

THE WORLD WOULD be very grateful to any psychiatrist who would make a statistical study comparing mental troubles and selfishness. Here it is assumed that the investigation would not concern itself with organic or physiological causes of mental troubles, but solely with egotism. It is interesting that in the English language the words "selfish" and "selfishness" were not known until about three hundred years ago. Shakespeare certainly does not dwell upon the idea. Could it be that the recent advent of the word in history corresponds in some way with an increase of that which it describes? As a sin, selfishness is as old as humanity, and has always been identified as undue love of self. An unknown author described selfishness in the following poem:

> I had a little tea party this afternoon at three.
> 'Twas very small — three guests in all — just I, myself and me.
> Myself ate all the sandwiches, while I drank all the tea.
> 'Twas also I who ate the pie, and passed the cake to me.

Selfishness does not mean that there is not to be a proper love of self. Our Blessed Lord told us: "Love thy neighbor as thyself" (Mt 19:19). God made "self" the standard by which the neighbor is to be loved. This could not be, if love of self did not have a legitimate basis. Selfishness is the love of the wrong self; that is, the self that is indifferent to the feeling and the interest and the safety of others. People are not selfish because they wish to earn enough to raise a family, but they are selfish if they consult only their own gains regardless of the losses that they may bring on others.

Richard Chenevix Trench tells the story of an architect who was ordered by the king of Egypt to build a high tower that would warn mariners of the dangerous rocks in the sea. The architect cut in large letters in the stone of this tower his own name. He then plastered over the carvings, and on the plaster in gold leaf wrote the name of the king, as if he were doing him honor. It was not long until the waves had washed away the plaster, and the only name that appeared was his own.

It is not unusual, therefore, to find that there are many who will apparently glorify others, even the King of Kings, but in their own selfish way they are gratifying their own self-love.

All selfishness is necessarily unhappiness. The self is too small a prison in which to relax. Caring only for self is very much like a serpent devouring its own tail. There is a parable told in India that indicates how selfishness defeats itself. A selfish fool was bequeathed a rice field. The first season the irrigation water ran through his field and made it fruitful, then overflowed into the neighbor's field and gave him blessing. But the next season the selfish fool said within himself: "Why should I let all of this water flow through my field into his? Water is wealth, and I must keep it." He then built a dam that prevented the water from flowing into his neighbor's yard; but he found that he had no crop. The irrigation water brought blessing only as it flowed, and when it became stagnant it bred a marsh and a swamp.

The cure for selfishness is a generous overflowing of whatever self possesses, either to neighbor or to God. Rich people miss so much happiness in life by accumulating more wealth, rather than by visiting poor lands and individually helping the starving and the sick in those areas. The neighbor should be helped because he or she is another self. . . .

* * *

Once I asked a missionary from one of the islands in the Pacific which was the greatest virtue of the people whom he helped there. He answered: "I can tell you their greatest virtue in terms of what they regard as their greatest vice, namely 'Kai-Po,' which is the sin of eating alone." Some of them would go without food for two or three days until they could find one with whom they could share their blessings.

In contrast, near a church in Warwickshire, England, is a stone on which is to be found the following inscription:

> *Here lies a miser who lived for himself*
> *And cared for nothing but gathering pelf,*
> *Now where he is or how he fares*
> *Nobody knows and nobody cares.*

On television once, there was an interview with a very rich man. Without any embarrassment, he said that he never gave anything to poor individuals, that he would stand on a sidewalk for a half hour hoping that some passerby would pick him up and he would not need to hire a taxi, and that in his magnificent home he had installed a pay telephone, in order that "my friends would not be embarrassed if they wanted to make a call."

Tolstoy told a beautiful story of a shoemaker who on the way home one night found a poor man shivering and poorly clad. Moved by pity, he took him home. But his wife complained about his bringing a stranger into the house and the cost of feeding another mouth. As she continued, the stranger grew smaller and smaller, shriveled and wrinkled with every unkind word. But when she spoke kindly to him and gave him food, he grew and became more beautiful. The reason was that the stranger was an angel from heaven in human form and could live only in an atmosphere of kindness and love.

The ungenerous soul has forgotten that everything he has came to him from God and that, acting as a trustee instead of an owner, he is one day to render an account of his stewardship. Furthermore, the more generous we are to others, the more merciful will be our own judgment. In driving home this lesson, Our Blessed Lord told the story of the one hundred sheep, the ten pieces of money, and the two sons — one of whom was a prodigal. One of the one hundred sheep was lost.

Upon finding it, the shepherd put it on his shoulders and brought it into the house; the other ninety-nine were left in the field. The woman who had ten pieces of money rejoiced more at finding the one that was lost than in the possession of the nine which were safe. The father was so happy at the return of the Prodigal Son that he killed a fatted calf. These are pictures of the mercy, kindness, and the forgiveness of God to those who, in their turn, are forgiving, generous, and merciful.

At what point are selfishness and greed turned into thoughtfulness of others? In a limited way when we become conscious that we are all brothers and sisters. In a higher way through the realization that having the great debt of our sins forgiven, we seek to relieve the debts of others. Such was the inspiration of Zaccheus, a dishonest tax collector, who climbed into a sycamore tree to see Our Divine Lord. Our Lord told him that He wanted to visit his house. The Divine forces Himself on no one; God withholds Himself from no one. God respects that awful prerogative that each one is the architect of his own good or evil, by free and unrestrained choice. Immediately after the visit, Zaccheus, recalling all his dishonesty, promised to pay back all that he had stolen and, in addition, to give generously to the poor.

The one thing that makes a complete revolution in the human soul, that changes selfishness into generosity, that upsets one's value of the dollar and makes a new man or woman, is the manifestation of the supreme love manifested in God, who came down to this earth to pay our debt of sin and rescue us from the swamp of selfishness that makes us so weak and frustrated.

* * *

Today charity is organized, which means that many are pinched and approached and cajoled until they give. Pressure methods may get more in modern philanthropy, but there is no greater betterment of the giver or the receiver than when one gives because one has been forgiven; we love in order to increase the eternal content of love in the world.

[THE POWER OF LOVE]

Courtesy

A GENERAL COMPLAINT heard by many in our times is the gradual disappearance of courtesy, politeness, and gentleness among people. There is no point in writing a lamentation about it; it is better to recall its true nature.

Courtesy is often regarded as a mere secular virtue due to gentle birth, high breeding, or affected social training. Its roots, however, are much deeper. As Hilaire Belloc wrote:

> Of Courtesy, it is much less
> Than Courage of Heart or Holiness,
> Yet in my walks it seems to me
> That the Grace of God is in Courtesy.

* * *

The divine injunction, "Do to others all that you would have them do to you" is not something negative in its encouragement of courtesy. It does not mean not leaving cigarette butts on the upholstery of Aunt Elsie's sofa because she may come and leave cigarette butts on your dining room chair. Rather, it is positive; namely, the doing of things to others such as you would like others to do to you. You would like them to remember you on your birthday, to write a note to you in your bereavement. It is a going out of our way to do nice things for people, whether they are nice or not.

Courtesy and good manners are the crowning beauty of consecrated conduct; it is seeing the worth in others, because they are God's creatures and because in their own souls they may be a thousand times more worthy of His blessing. Everyone in the world carries around with him a certain moral atmosphere, which to a great extent determines his relations to fellow creatures. A beautiful woman who becomes insanely jealous of another beautiful woman and insults her has about her that fetid air of egotism that diffuses itself in the bad smell of discourtesy. Courtesy in its roots is saintliness; that is why sometimes one will find it in the most unlettered and uneducated, such as in the simple peasants in Europe; in such cases, there is often a gentleness that far surpasses the effete and superficial manners of the educated.

Goethe was right when he said, "There is no outward sign of courtesy that does not rest on a deep moral foundation." Courtesy is love in action; not the love that seeks to be loved in return, but the love that puts affection in others, and finds them lovable.

[THE POWER OF LOVE]

Love may be defined as mutual self-giving and self-outpouring which ends in self-recovery.

[HYMN OF THE CONQUERED]

The Philosophy
of Charity

T HERE IS A PHILOSOPHY behind charity as there is a philosophy
behind everything else in life. It is that philosophy in relation
to the tendencies in modern social service that this chapter
seeks to discover and analyze in the light of Catholic philosophy.

The first tendency in modern charity, if we are correctly observ-
ing contemporary movement, is toward greater organization, even to
the extent of making it one of the big business concerns of the country. The bread-basket stage, the penny-in-a-tin-cup stage, the handout
stage, have given way to the bureau and the scientific-giving stage.
Statistics are replacing sympathy, and social workers are replacing
emotions.

The complexities of modern life, the crisscrossing of economic and
personal factors, demand a discipline in giving, and a skill in investigation, that can be attained only by the organized effort of those specially
trained in such work and thoroughly conversant with such conditions.
Whether or not this tendency is a desirable one is at present not the
point at issue. It is the facts we are seeking, and to elaborate further the
obviousness of the tendency toward organization would be only gilding
the lily.

The second tendency in modern charity is toward a deification of society at the expense of the individual. The philosophical principle behind this tendency is not that of the common good, which claims that individuals shall effectively cooperate for the well-being of society, but rather the principle that individuals should be submerged for the sake of the collectivity. In a text well known to social workers, one finds such a philosophy in these words: "Human nature itself is now regarded as a product of social intercourse" — which statement implies that society creates human nature, rather than that human nature creates society. Of the same mind, another sociologist carries glorification of society to the detriment of the individual to such a height that he makes "the service of God consist in the service of men," and consequently denies any such thing as an individual sin. The only sin is the social sin: "disloyalty to society."

The final tendency in modern philanthropy is toward absoluteness — not in the sense that it seeks to rid the world of poverty, crime, and disease, but in the sense that the alleviation or partial elimination of these ills constitutes its full and final purpose. Giving bread means filling empty stomachs — it means nothing more, and it can mean nothing more. Improving home conditions means better sunlight, better food, warmer temperature — and nothing more. There is no other purposiveness behind social work than the tangible, and no other finality than the eradication from society of the "d's" — dependents, defectives, and delinquents.

Any vision beyond that which can be embraced in a budget or compiled statistically or touched by hands is regarded as a form of idealism to which these philanthropists feel a positive antipathy. It is assumed throughout the whole process of alleviating the ills of humankind that humanity has no other destiny than the present, and that the fruits of helpfulness and philanthropy, if they extend beyond a stomach, a playground, or a clinic, never go any further than a formula gleaned from those experiences.

If our finger has been properly kept on the pulse of modern philanthropy, it would seem to indicate a triple condition or tendency:

1. A tendency toward organization as regards its *form;*

2. A tendency toward the hypersocial at the expense of the individual as regards its *method;*

3. A tendency toward the absolute as regards its *purpose.*

Now, what interpretation does the traditional philosophy of charity bring to these tendencies? Does it disapprove them, does it approve them, or does it inject a new spirit into them and consequently transform them? Catholic thought is essentially a transforming thought, elevating the baser things to higher planes in the hierarchy of values, thanks to its power of divine alchemy.

The true philosophy of charity would not condemn these modern tendencies and ask their destruction. Rather, it would ask that they be elevated to conform to these three principles:

1. Charity must not only be organized, but must also be organic;

2. Charity must deal not only with society but also with individual souls;

3. Charity must not be absolute, but sacramental, i.e., not only of the earth earthy but of the heavens heavenly.

The assumption behind organized charity is that charity work becomes organized when individuals come together and unite themselves for the purpose of remedying the social ills of humanity, as people might come together and form a club. It is further assumed that charity work develops horizontally, that is, it begins with people and ends with people, proceeding from the organization through the social worker and finally out to the needy. There is thought to be no difference in kind, but only one of degree, between the will of the person, which calls the organization into being, and the poor disorganized people who receive the fruits of the organization.

This conception of charity is not the Christ-like one. For Judeo-Christians, the source of charity is not the will of others, but the will of God. The origin of charity lies not in effective human groupings but in divine life, and hence its development or unfolding is not horizontal, like the history of human institutions, which begin with people and end with people, but vertical, beginning with God at its summit, and ending with man as its term. . . .

*   *   *

Charity, then, is not organized, nor is charity work accomplished through organizations. An organization is an assembly of people for the better securing of a particular object, but there is no intrinsic connection between the controlling head of an organization and its members. Charity is organic, in the sense that it belongs to an organism in which there is a vital connection between the cells or members that make it up, and a vital connection as well between the head and the body, as in the human organism. Charity may embrace a grouping of persons, records, statistics, committees, graphs, and budgets. It may be these, but something more; it is organic — organic because alive with the life of a body; organic because the flesh and blood of its members are the living members of the body of Christ. . . .

*   *   *

It is our contention that society is not a new being but only a new *mode of being.* Society is made up of like elements, not unlike ones. Adding drops of water to drops of milk does not make water, but milk and water. So too adding individual to individual does not constitute a thing separate, distinct, from the individuals, but only a new modality of the individuals' existences.

Society does not destroy individuals, nor can it exist apart from individuals. It has no unitary consciousness, it being only the resultant of the functional coordination of individuals in an organic whole. And this doctrine of common sense finds further verification in Revelation. The Church or the incarnate charity of Jesus Christ, it has been said, is an organism, a body made up of many members. Now we hasten to add that just as the life of a human organism does not destroy the individual cell-life of its millions of cells, so neither does the mystical body of Christ destroy the individuality of the members. We all share the individual life of Christ, and yet there is no absorption, no merging of offices; there still remains diversity of ministries but the same spirit. There is unity, but there is also multiplicity.

If society in the natural order, or the mystical body in the supernatural, does not absorb, submerge, or swallow up the individual, it follows that the talk about "social processes," "social prevision," "humanitarianism," is beside the point. The problems of social work may be stated in the abstract, but *practically* the solution must touch an individual and an individual who has certain inviolable rights.

Juvenile delinquency, for example, is ultimately the problem of the young delinquent; crime is a problem of the criminal; tuberculosis, a problem of the tubercular; poverty, a problem of the poor man or poor woman; flood-relief, a problem neither of the flood nor of relief but of a victim. And so we might go on, always keeping in the back of our heads the sound principle that there is no such thing as humanity; there are only Peters and Pauls, Marys and Anns. And according to Christian doctrine, each of these has an individual soul. Hence social service is dealing not with *something* but *somebody*.

Over and over again the Church insists that the least of the individuals, such as the poor human earthenware that is thrown into our gutters and those with focusless eyes who bat their heads against padded cells, are infinitely worth saving because they were infinitely worth redeeming. And any form of philanthropy that forgets the doctrine of the common good for the false principle that society is a new entity for which individuals must be sacrificed, sooner or later will be advocating elimination of the unfit....

There may be much in humanity that is worth loving, even from human motives, but there is little to love from human motives in the wrecks that come to charities. If there is to be love for them, it must be inspired by Someone Who first loved someone who was not worth loving — I mean Christ loving us — and unless the social worker sees Christ in the needy, he or she will not long love the needy.

The true philosophy of charity cannot accept without correctives the modern tendency to regard as the absolute end of charity the alleviation of the ills that afflict humanity, nor can it regard as an ideal a society that is free from disease, hospitals, and prisons — not because such an ideal is wrong, but because it is incomplete.

It is a tenet of the Catholic philosophy of charity that the lessening of human ills and the diminution of the traces of disease are not ends in themselves, but rather means to an end....

*   *   *

Charity, in brief, centers about two realities: human natures, who dispense or receive benefices; and things, like gold and silver, clothing and food. Charity embraces in its scope both what we are and what we have....

Such is the philosophy of Catholic charity, and since the day charity became organic with us, it has never been quite right to say that God is in His heaven and all's right with world; for Christ has left the heavens to set it right, and is found among us, even as we talk.

[OLD ERRORS AND NEW LABELS]

Charity is a quality of the soul, rather than an isolated good deed.

[PREFACE TO RELIGION]

A Thousand Tiny Delicacies

POLITENESS IS A WAY of showing externally the internal regard we have for others. Good manners are the shadows cast by virtues. As the spoken word is the audible sign of an idea we have in our mind, so politeness is a telltale arid token of reverence for others in our own spirit. Politeness differs from etiquette in two ways: Etiquette can be a pose, a posture, or an air that is put on like a garment; politeness is a habit of the soul. Second, etiquette has certain rules for special occasions, such as what to do when you drop a fork under the table. On the contrary, politeness is a spirit that suffuses all situations and meets the requirements of a given situation without any specific rule to cover the case.

One wonders if politeness and courtesy have declined in our civilization. Schools do not teach courtesy, and there are some homes that do not. But politeness never loses its hold on society, because of the goodness and greatness of some souls. It is said of George Washington that many would slap him on the shoulder and call him "George." Yet he took off his hat and bowed his head to an old slave who first took off his hat, saying, "Good morning, General Washington." General Lafayette, who was in the company of Washington at the time, asked him why he bowed to the slave. The answer was, "I would not permit him to be a better gentleman than I!"

One of the elements of courtesy would certainly be attention to details in kindliness to others. The human heart is more satisfied with a thousand tiny delicacies scattered through the days and years than one sudden outburst and costly token of esteem, thereafter lapsing into forgetfulness and indifference. Our Divine Lord promised that those who would be put over the great things were those who were faithful in the little things. Boaz of Old Testament history was a man who not only greeted with courtesy, but also gave a blessing to the workers in his fields. Then he instructed the gleaners purposely to leave some of the sheaves after them that Ruth might have what she desired. His thoughtfulness extended not just to heroic sacrifice, but to trivial donations.

The courteous person will always give more than the law requires. Therefore, courtesy can manifest itself not only in trivialities but also in excesses. Judged by external standards, the widow's mite was too little a contribution to the temple, just as the penitent's costly ointment was too much in the eyes of a moneygrubber. But both had in them that inner generosity that is the essence of love's excess of the law. Courtesy, it would seem, must also be what St. Paul described as "love without hypocrisy." Love is to courtesy what the soul is to the body. Without it, we have formalism and stiffness but no real politeness. Courtesy is affection and not affectation. It reaches a point where, in a true lowliness of mind, one esteems others better than self. We know the worst that is in us and of that we can be certain, but we can never know the worst that is in others; we can at best only suspect it. Conscious of this, our feelings toward others become delicate and sensitive; they may even become deeply religious when they reach a point where we forgive others their discourtesies. This is done because we know that God Himself has forgiven our greater transgressions.

Politeness is not a sign of weakness when it is love without hypocrisy; it is a sign of strength because it involves considerable self-control on our part. Its root is sympathy, and sympathy is based on a consciousness of the natural order of our membership in the human race and our fellowship in the spiritual order with the redeemed sons and daughters of God. The unsympathetic person is never courteous.

St. Francis of Assisi explained it well: "Courtesy is one of the properties of God Who gives His sun and rain to the just and the unjust by courtesy; and courtesy is the sister of charity by which hatred is extinguished and love is cherished."

[ON BEING HUMAN]

Courtesy is not a condescension of a superior to an inferior, or a patronizing interest in another's affairs. It is the homage of the heart to the sacredness of human worth.

[THOUGHTS FOR DAILY LIVING]

The Problem of Giving

"T O HAVE" is the opposite of "to give," yet each of these things is good in its proper place. To have is to extend our personalities: We do not contain within ourselves all the essentials for human living, therefore our "being" must be completed by also "having." Existence implies the right to have sufficient food and clothing and a place to live; it does not, however, imply the right to have a seagoing yacht. Our rights to own property, to have things, decrease as the objects are further and further removed from personal necessities.

The virtue of giving is dependent upon having, for unless we possess something, we cannot give it away. (This is true even of our time.) But having does not, to most people, appear as an opportunity for giving — they look upon giving as a loss, because having is, in itself, so dear to them. This is shortsighted; if you give away half a loaf, another half loaf remains to you, and you have had the happiness of being a donor too.

Many people, especially among the rich, estimate the value of their own personalities in terms of owning more and more unessential things. They refuse to cut into their capital, increasing it each year until it seems to them another self without which they would not be complete. To slice off a portion of this capital through alms would seem to them like cutting off an arm or a leg.

One woman has lived in history because she did not fear cutting into her capital. The story is told in the gospel: "As He was sitting opposite the treasury of the temple, Jesus watched the multitude throwing coins into the treasury, the many rich with their offerings; and there was one poor widow, who came and put in two mites, which makes a farthing. Thereupon He called his disciples to Him, and said to them, 'Believe me, this poor widow has put in more than all those others who have put offerings into the treasury. The others all gave out of what they had to spare; she, with so little to give, put in all that she had, her whole livelihood' " (Mt 12:41–44).

Our Divine Lord was interested in studying the almsgivers, and it was the quality of their giving that arrested Him far more than the quantity they gave. He had once said that where our treasure is, there our heart is also. Now He tells us that where the heart goes, there the treasure follows. Few of us have His attitude toward alms; we do not trouble to read the list of donors in fine type under the heading, "Amounts less than..." But probably that would be to Him the most important section of the list. On that occasion in the temple He immortalized a gift of two of the smallest coins in the ancient world.

Probably the poor woman at the temple did not see her Judge or know that she had pleased Him, or guess that, in the scales of divine justice, she gave more than all those others who put offerings into the treasury. They gave of their superfluity; she gave all she had, "her whole livelihood." She was poor, yet she gave to the poor. She emptied herself to fill the emptiness of others. The jingle of her two small coins as they fell cried out to refute the whole base philosophy of materialism, which would teach everyone to acquire as they can — as if this earth were our only home.

And the widow's tiny gift has another meaning: It reminds us that Our Lord wants everything from us. He was the first "totalitarian" of the spirit: He asks that we hold nothing back from Him. He demands total love: "With thy whole mind, thy whole heart, thy whole spirit, and thy whole strength." Only those who have given their whole hearts to God can give Him their whole capital as well.

Nothing that is given in such a spirit of generosity is ever lost. In the materialist's reckoning, what is renounced is lost forever. In the realm of the spirit, this is not true. For what we give to God is not only recorded to us for eternal merit — it is even returned in this life. One of the most practical ways of assuring that we shall always have enough is to give and give and give in the name of the Lord. Similarly, the most rapid increase in love of God can be obtained by being totally generous to our neighbors. "Give and the gifts will be yours; good measure, pressed down and shaken up and running over, will be poured into your lap; the measure you award to others is the measure that will be awarded to you" (Lk 6:39).

The use to which we put what we have is closely related to what we are, to our "being," and to what we will become. Those who keep everything they have for themselves must lose it all at death; those who have given it away will get it back in the coin of immortality and joy.

[ON BEING HUMAN]

"Write a check!" This is one of the most common expressions of people who are called generous and philanthropic, when asked to subscribe for a cause, or to build a field house or a laboratory. They discharge the appeal by a stroke of the pen. While this immediacy of giving is very much to be commended, and while it never fails to rejoice the recipient, there is often wanting a spiritual quality that affects both the check writer and the check endorser. This is particularly true of very large donations. Andrew Carnegie, who gave away millions, once said that he never missed anything that he gave away; first, because he did not know how much he had; second, because all that he gave away was paper, and he could never notice any decrease in his paper, by which he meant checks, stocks, bonds, etc.

[WHAT GOOD AM I DOING HERE?]

Caring for Humanity

WHEN AMORIZATION of humanity becomes personal, it is caring. But caring can be difficult if there is inferiority or superiority.

Not having had time for lunch, one afternoon I stepped into a small grocery store to buy a box of crackers for a snack. As I entered, I saw a mother in the back of her store with a four-year-old child who had just pulled a bottle of vinegar off the shelf, breaking it into pieces. Standing over him, she said repeatedly, "Pick up those pieces!" With each command, he became more rebellious. It was evident that she would have loved to have slapped him, but she dared not because she wanted to appear compassionate before the customers. The father, waiting on them, enjoyed his neutrality, ignoring both the case of the mother and the son. However, it was very evident that as she was thinking, "The boy is just like his father, stubborn and self-willed," he was thinking, "Just like his mother's family, always making a show of authority."

The mother, leaving the spilled vinegar and broken pieces of glass on the floor, finally dragged her son off to a back room, as a child might drag a rag doll. Who won the battle? Was it the child who maintained his will through tears, for tears are the last refuge of the weak? Or was it the mother who seemingly renounced her strength, though it was evident she was forced to capitulate?

Here we are faced with a problem that has very well been summarized by Dr. Jean de Rougemont: "If my neighbor is stronger than I am, I fear him; if he is weaker than I am, I despise him. If he is equal to me, I use subterfuge and find excuses for either asserting my superiority or for not obeying him."

The strong and the weak! Superiority and inferiority! The same tension exists in the rich helping the poor. Do the rich help the poor because of a kind of pity, which makes the poor feel their inferiority? Do the poor in their turn resent being helped by the rich, because it offends their dignity and degrades their personality by being made dependent? Do the rich maintain a kind of equality by helping only the rich, and the poor maintain theirs by helping the poor? An institution that is already worth $100 million can easily get another $150 million. Thus the rich keep on their level by enriching the rich — they also get an honorary doctorate at commencement exercises and tickets on the fifty-yard line at one of the football games.

Those with little, on the contrary, generally help the poor, for here there is a deeper sympathy and understanding of what another suffers. It is very likely that the rich man in the parable of Lazarus wrote out very large checks to philanthropic causes, but he probably drew his curtains whenever a funeral procession passed by and avoided the exit where Lazarus sat with his sores.

HOW SOLVE THE PROBLEM?

How solve this problem of the strong and the weak, the rich and the poor, with weak fearing the strong and the strong despising the weak? The real solution is not to be found in any kind of law, for law ignores personal dialogue with others and also secures its right by imposing penalties. Then, too, there can be a respect for neighbor, because it happens to be a mood or a fashion, rather than an upsurge of love. There should be some other way to care for others that is not like a plastic flower pinned to a barren tree, but rather a blossom that grows out of the tree itself.

As the distinguished psychiatrist Paul Tournier has pointed out: The strong must see their own weakness; the weak must see their own poverty; the poor must see their own wealth; the learned must see their ignorance; the ignorant must see their peculiar kind of wisdom.

Let the strong ask themselves: *How strong am I?* Am I master and captain of my soul, or am I driven about by every wind of passion? How long have I been able to stay on a diet? Or on the wagon? What New Year's resolution have I kept? Have I not resolved as a mother to be kinder to my children — and yet blast them even when I take aspirin for my nerves? Am I strong enough to cut down to one pack of cigarettes a day, as I wish I could? Can I resist flying off the handle when someone in the office crosses me? Can I resist a second or third cocktail when I know that it causes me to make everyone in the office uncomfortable? How strong am I in resisting lust or dishonesty?

How *rich* am I when I look at the poverty of my inner life? I may *have* something, but *am* I anything? Am I not poverty-stricken as regards self-mastery, and, oh, how rich in egotism and selfishness! How wise am I? I may know all the Books of the Month, being proud of my college education, but have I ever discovered the meaning of life? Is there anything lovable in me at all? Am I not nasty and cranky? Do I not short-circuit every conversation with a fellow worker at the water cooler?

But I still love myself. I am good to myself. I give myself a good chair when I come into the room. I always order the best food, avoiding anything that does not flatter my palate. I avoid conversations that might embarrass me.

If then I can love myself, despite all of my weaknesses, failures, and faults, why can I not love my neighbor, despite all of his or her faults? If I am really not rich at all, except on the outside, but inwardly poor, then why can I not really love the poor, who are richer on the inside than I? Why can I not love others, despite the way they are?

THE STRONG SEEING THEIR WEAKNESS

Here is the answer to how the strong can avoid despising the weak and the rich humiliating the poor: The strong must see their own ignorance.

Our Divine Lord said, "Love your neighbor as yourself." Why did He not say, Love your neighbor *more* than yourself? Because when we see how much we love ourselves, despite the fact that we are unlovable, then the greatest love we can show our neighbors is to love them despite their unlovableness. How many there are who say they hate themselves. But do they really? Let anyone else tell them how hateful they are, and they flare up in love for themselves.

But over and above all this, I am loved by God despite all my faults, failures, and infidelities. There is nothing in me that should make me lovable to God. Then why does He love me? Because He puts some of His love into me. He loves me as a mother loves a child with a dirty face; her image is in the child, and it is this the mother sees and loves. If then I, who am not worth loving, am loved by Love, the least I can do for others is to do what God has done for me. Once I no longer regard myself as a superman, who refuses to share the struggle of others, then when others are weak, I am weak; when they are poor, I am poor; when they are tearful, my cheeks are damp. Then I see not that I am loved because God loves everybody; but rather that, if God loves me, as miserable as I am, then He *must love everybody.*

Only when I am as weak and helpless as my neighbor can I help him. Then there is no spirit of judgment, no sense of superiority, no superciliousness, no looking down one's nose at others. I am his companion in repentance. I too am waiting for grace, just as he did.

We notice how much intimacy this creates with another when a patient is faced with a serious operation. If a doctor tells a patient that an operation is necessary, the patient becomes frightened at the prospect. If, however, the doctor says, "I have had this operation," then the patient has an assurance that is based upon true sympathy. Only those who have been wounded really know how to bind up wounds.

From another point of view, are not the hearts of the strong and the chivalrous captured by weakness that solicits defense? Every language uses the diminutive to express tenderness, even to such a thing as a baby elephant. Beauty is bound up with the petite, not generally with the fat. There is a greater love of chicks than of chickens, of lambs than of sheep, of puppies than dogs, of kittens than cats.

LOVE IS THE REASON

One moves out of the realm of rights, law, civic equality, as soon as one is governed by love. It changes not only ourselves; it changes others.

Once there was a girl born of parents who constantly quarreled and made her feel that she was unwanted as she was certainly unloved. They finally separated. She had to shift for herself in a world that was a kind of jungle. She had no faith in those whom she met. She did not even have faith in herself. The rough, coarse ways of her home seemed to have left their mark and made her unhappy on the outside and afraid of others.

Then one day a miracle happened. She met a young man who came from loving parents. Despite all of the seeming commonness of the young woman, he saw her basically sweet manner and a potential for devotion and dedication. Her life completely changed in a moment. She was loved, appreciated, and cared for! She suddenly realized that she was beautiful, not because she had ever thought she was, but because he loved her. A song asks whether a young woman is loved because she is beautiful or is she beautiful because she is loved. The true beauty is that which is created by love — the kind of love that cares, that never seems superior, is creative, making the other person a true self, even nobler than self.

A wealthy American visiting one of our leper colonies in the Pacific came across a nun who was caring for about three hundred lepers and said to her, "Sister, I wouldn't do that for a million dollars." She said, "Neither would I."

A woman visiting a neighbor said, "I would give my life to have two children like that." The mother answered, "That is exactly what it costs." That much love, that much life, that much care!

CONCERN

It has been said that happiness is a twin, which means that we are really never happy unless we share. We were made for openness to the world. Our five senses put us in contact with the universe; our intellect enables us to understand it. Some, indeed, cut themselves off deliberately from its science, its culture, its music, impoverishing their joys and hardening themselves to the thrill of knowing. We cannot exist without Encounter or without Care, which is a responsible being reacting to others, thus helping others to grow and develop. Fellowship or humanity is the matrix womb of our existence; we were born out of it — the family, the nation, the world. To it we return, to become whole and even normal. A character in the novel of Johan Bojer, mindful of his ties to impoverished humanity, says, "Here I am, for instance, sitting among clean people and eating with a silver fork at my table with a white cloth, and yet — well, I can't quite manage to feel only joy and gladness over it all, for half my inner consciousness is with the thousands that at this moment haven't even salt for the soup."

WE ARE ALL PART OF HUMANITY

Albert Camus, in his work *The Plague*, described a city whose hotel was ridden by rats, thus frightening the entire population:

> "Are our city fathers aware that the decaying bodies of these rodents constitute a grave danger to the population?"
> The manager of the hotel can talk of nothing else, but he has a personal grievance too — that a dead rat should be found in the elevator of a three-star hotel seems to him the end of all things. To console him, I said: "But you know everybody is in the same

boat." "That's just it," he replied. "Now, we're like everybody else."

It was hell to him to be like everybody else. He refused to see himself a part of the muck and mud, the poverty and the starvation of all his brothers. He wanted to be different, alone, isolated — which in the end would make him frustrated. Every self-centered person is a self-disrupted person. Nothing has *happened* to him — he *did* something to himself: He no longer cared.

CARING AS A THERAPY

Egotists do not need psychiatrists, though patients with true psychoses and neuroses do. The egotistic are always out of sorts with themselves and with others. Instead of turning to others in care, they turn to themselves in self-pity. A house divided against itself cannot stand....

*   *   *

In the play *Peer Gynt*, the hero visits a lunatic asylum where he believes that people are out of their minds or out of themselves. The director corrects him: "It's here that men are most themselves — themselves and nothing but themselves — sailing without spread sails of self. Each shuts himself in a cask of self, the cask stopped with the bung of self and seasoned in a well of self. None has tears for others' woes, or cares what any other thinks."

The cure for this general malady of selfishness is to break out of our walled garden or glass cage. Existence is not opaque and unrelated to the universe and people about us. Existence has a relatedness to every-thing. That is why there is in us a nostalgia, a sense of nonfulfillment, until we complete it by having an encounter with others. Care makes one a responsible being, reacting to others, helping others grow and develop.

There is not a frustrated egotist who could not be cured by get-ting his back off a couch, getting on his feet to serve. His weakness would pass out through his fingers in what might be called the therapy of touch. Instead of having his guilt explained away, he could work it away with a love that covers a multitude of sins.

A British psychiatrist, Maxwell Jones, introduced into a hospital what he called community care. The project was that each person should have contact with those either in the same room or, if he was ambulatory, on the same floor; he was to consider himself a part of the healing community. No one was to talk about his illness but to bring solace to others. The orderlies, the nurses, the doctors, also pledged themselves to be interested in others. Three results followed: Patients recovered more quickly, because they were loved. Doctors discovered that fewer formal interviews with patients were necessary, because of the new form of care on the part of the patients. Third, the doctor divested himself of unnecessary symbols of authority, such as the white coat and the stethoscope, and depended upon earning his status as a real person in the life of the patients and the personnel.

It is all very well and good to release people from certain anxieties, but the real cure does not come until one is released *to* a concern for the welfare of others. The cruelest words of tongue or pen are, "I could not have cared less." The ungiven self is an unfulfilled self.

SYMPATHY

One wonders if there is not more sympathy in smaller communities than in great cities. One can live in apartments and not know the next-door neighbor, but there is hardly a village in which one does not know the next-door neighbor. There is probably less borrowing of sugar in all of the apartments of New York than there is in a village of five hundred. Not long ago, a picture magazine took photographs for one hour of people who passed by a wounded man on a subway stair. The magazine recounted in pictures the number who looked at the man and then went on their way without making a sympathetic inquiry. But the magazine itself forgot to state that the photographer was more interested in the click of his machine than he was in the tick of the heart of the wounded man.

This does not mean to say that sympathy is nonexistent, for the generous heart of Americans pours itself out in alms and in sympathy to the needy and the poor.

Sympathy is a temper or character that draws others together. It is what might be called conductivity. The Greek origin of the word "sympathy" implies "suffering with." It is a kind of silent understanding when heart meets heart. It is a kind of substitution, in which one takes the heart out of his or her own body and places it in the body of another person, and in exchange takes back the other's heart. It is not mere pity, for pity can be like the traveler in the gospel who looked on the wounded man but did not help. Sentimentality can exist in low souls, but pure sympathy resides only in the noble.

Sometimes sympathy can be silent, particularly where there is grief. St. Paul told the Romans: "Weep with those that weep." The shedding of a common tear is far more eloquent than are honeyed words. This is well-proved in the case of Job, whose comforters sat silently seven days beside him; their consolation was far greater than when they broke their silence and gave so many false reasons as to why Job suffered.

The foundation of all true sympathy, and that which makes it universal, is love. The best of people can offer only human tenderness without understanding the mystery of pain and tears. But when one comes to the love of Christ, one finds both the tenderness of the human and the comprehensiveness of the Divine. In Him alone is united sympathy and the understanding of the mystery of pain. It was that that made Him weep over the death of His beloved friend Lazarus. Many people have a heart, but they lack the mind to embrace the mystery.

Hence, the Lord bade us to have sympathy with all people, not in the way of condescension, not as the pure lifting their skirts from the impure; but as people touching to heal, as people hating the sin and loving the sinner....

* * *

The nature of giving is best illustrated in the life of Our Blessed Lord, Who one day was approached by a leper who asked for healing. The gospel tells us that Our Lord stretched forth His Hand and touched the leper. Jesus could have healed without the touch, as He healed the servant of the centurion at a distance. Why then, in the face of one of life's greatest miseries and a disease from which the healthy often recoil, did the Lord cure with a touch?

Because of a spiritual quality in the Giver — namely, compassion or the ability to suffer with others. Touch is the language of love. There are actually three intimacies in love: hearing, seeing, and touching. We could never love anyone unless we first know him or hear his voice. Next, after hearing a voice, one wishes to see the person. Vision is the second intimacy. Then finally, there comes the greatest of all intimacies, which only a few may enjoy, and that is the intimacy of touch.

The Son of God made Man touched the leper in order to annihilate distance between the Giver and the receiver, between the Lover and the beloved, to prove sympathy by contact, to identify Himself with the woes of others. How different was the attitude of Shylock, who said, "I will buy with you, sell with you, talk with you, walk with you, . . . but I will not eat with you, drink with you, nor pray with you."

[FOOTPRINTS IN A DARKENED FOREST]

Modern Saints

GANDHI

For Gandhi, the *contemplata* was nonviolence to others with violence to self. When asked to take part in a war of independence, he answered, "I decline to take part in it; today I am teaching the people how to meet a national crisis by nonviolent means." But the sword that he refused to swing against others, he thrust into his own flesh.

Christianity and Hinduism have something in common — namely, the value of asceticism, self-denial, and renunciation. Neither of them glorifies self-renunciation as such. St. Paul said that if he should deliver his body to be burned and have no love, it was useless. Gandhi also, in the same spirit, said, "A mother would never by choice sleep in a wet bed; but she would gladly do so, in order to spare the dry bed for her child." Renunciation was never to be for its own sake but for the sake of others.

One of the first steps toward the crushing of the ego, in order to make himself available to others, was Gandhi's taking of the vow of celibacy when he was thirty-seven years old, which vow he kept until his death in 1948. Celibacy in the Hindu lore was called *bramacharya*, which is a complete self-control that ruled out uncleanness, lying, hate, and anger, and made one like to God because less self-centered. This abandonment of the pleasures of the flesh, he believed, would make his love for his fellowmen more free and outreaching.

Another form of self-renunciation that helped him identify himself with others through de-egotism was fasting. Gandhi claimed that prayer united us to God, while fasting separated us from an excessive love of creatures. The fast, he claimed, was a means of reaching people's hearts and minds: "I fasted to reform those who loved me. You cannot fast against a tyrant, for a tyrant is incapable of love." His fasting was often for the sake of the Untouchables, who were not permitted to enter a Hindu temple and inhabited the worst of the slums and villages. His fasting, which identified him with the starving, helped to win equality for the Untouchables.

Gandhi embraced Christ, but rejected Christianity. He had a black-and-white print of Christ hanging in his little hut, on which was written: "He is our Peace." Gandhi said, "If I had to face only the Sermon on the Mount in my own interpretation of it, I should unhesitatingly say, 'Yes, I am a Christian.'"

Anyone in public life has burdens. St. Paul spoke of bearing on his shoulders the burden of all the churches. Gandhi bore the emptiness of India's starving millions.

POPE JOHN

The mystique of Pope John XXIII was the love of God and the love of neighbor. There are some who love neighbor without loving God, but such love reaches limits beyond which it refuses to humble itself for another. One soldier, during the last war, boasted, "I am glad I am an atheist. If I were a Christian, I would have to help those dysentery patients." Those who love God without loving neighbor have a heart that keeps all the blood for itself, refusing to send it to the extremities. Pope John's deep and all-encompassing love of humanity came from his love of God: "I am like every other man in the world. I have been blessed with a disposition to love mankind, which keeps me faithful to the teachings of the Gospel, makes me respectful of my rights and the rights of others, and which prevents me from doing evil to anyone. In fact, it encourages me to do good to everyone."

This accounted for his perpetual good humor. When he was patriarch of Venice, a high tide flooded the Piazza di San Marco; to escape the rising waters, he went into a small wineshop. The man behind the counter recognized him and stammered out, "Dry throat, Eminence?" He shook his head and said, "No, wet feet." I visited with him in company with Yousuf Karsh, the famous photographer. Pope John said, "God knew from all eternity that I was destined to be Pope. He also knew that I would live for over eighty years. Having all eternity to work on, and also eighty years, wouldn't you think He would have made me better looking?"

This love of humanity also begot in him a profound humility and a resistance to ever considering himself above others. Though he was a cardinal before he was named Pope, he refused to be a cardinal in the sense of being an Eminence, for "eminence" is taken from the Latin word *entinens*, which means "far off." The origin of this elevation began in 1244, when Margaret, Countess of Flanders, visited Pope Innocent IV, who had just been elected the previous year in Rome. She was the daughter of Baldwin II, the Latin emperor of Constantinople. She was gently chided in the course of the visit to the Pontiff, because she seemed to address everyone alike, justifying herself, "How is it possible to tell an abbot from a cardinal? They all dress in black." The Pontiff asked her, "Well, what would you suggest?" She said, "I would suggest giving them red hats."

The red hat John never took very seriously, for immediately after his elevation he made a retreat in which he wrote in his notebook: "It costs me nothing to acknowledge and repeat that I am nothing and worth precisely nothing."

That love of humanity also came out in his famous encyclical *Mater et Magistra*, in which he pleaded for a socialization of humanity but not socialism. Socialism, he said, destroys the work of personality by absorption into the mass, but socialization "is at one and the same time an effect and a cause of growing intervention of public authorities in even the most crucial matters, such as those concerning the care of health, the instruction and edification of the younger generation, and the controlling of professional careers and the methods of care and rehabilitation of those variously handicapped. But it is also the fruit and expression of a natural tendency, almost irrepressible in human beings — the tendency to join together to attain objectives which are beyond the capacity and the means of single individuals."

This love of humanity had its even greater expression in the opening of the doors of the Church to let in the world and also to let the Church out. The purpose was to end the division in Christendom that has lasted in one instance over four hundred years and in another instance over seven hundred. On the day of his coronation, when he stood outside the doors of St. Peter's and bade the whole world to come to him, his great arms were like fleshy columns of Bernini, embracing all humanity and forever reminding the children of God that we are all brothers and sisters.

[FOOTPRINTS IN A DARKENED FOREST]

The humble person makes room for progress; the proud person believes he is already there.

[ON BEING HUMAN]

SPIRIT

"Aye" or "Nay" to Eternal Destiny

OFTEN THOSE WHO COMPLAIN that they receive "no breaks" in life are the very ones who have not utilized their gifts. It is true that there is a diversity of talents, some being given ten, others five, and others only one; but condemnation in the gospel is meted out only to those who do not make returns on their gift. This is because we are not merely receptive beings; we are also active. A lake, unless the living waters flow through it, becomes stagnant and putrid like the Dead Sea. The sun shines to light a world. The fleeting streams flow self-content by seeking out the ocean. The tree yields its fruit, the air ministers to life by passing through the lungs. Nature knows no arresting hand, no selfhood.

Gifts can be perverted and turned to disloyal uses, but they can also be neglected through personal ease and indulgence. Those who have not received many gifts sometimes undervalue them with perilous modesty, forgetting that the weakest vessel can hold some water, the simplest speech can praise the Lord, a stupid ass carried Him into Jerusalem.

The muscle that is not used atrophies. The UN reports an increase of certain diseases in the underprivileged nations because of malnutrition. But what of the privileged nations? Among these, there is an increase of coronary thrombosis, which is attributed in part to excessive fat and want of exercise. Minds are underdeveloped because they will not put forth the energy necessary to bring them to the joy and thrill of knowledge.

In the gospel, the one who is perpetually condemned is the one who does nothing with his gifts. It was so in the case of the priest and the Levite who passed by the wounded man on the road from Jerusalem to Jericho; it was so of the rich man, of whom no ill is recorded except that a beggar lay at his gate full of sores, and yet no one gave him to eat; it was true of the servant who hid in a napkin the talent committed to him; and also of the unprofitable servant who had only done what it was his duty to do. Someone plants a tree in order that it might bring forth fruit. The tree in the gospel that bore no fruit was ordered cut down because it only cumbered the ground. God expects returns for His great and wonderful investments in us. The condemned person is the negative person who gives way to the inertia of the moment, follows the line of least resistance, remains stunted, starved, and profitless to society.

The law of nature and of grace is inexorable in this matter of neglect. Those who have the capacity to learn and waste their time on mental pastry eventually reach a point where they cannot read a good book or absorb a spiritual inspiration — not because it lacks interest, but because it cannot interest them. People may sin away the very capacity even to desire the thing they need; they can even atrophy the ability to pray. Macbeth knew what he should pray for; words were not wanting, thoughts were not wanting, but in his soul he knew that he did not wish for the very thing he ought to pray for, because he had killed the power of a better affection and aspiration.

The most serious neglect is that of soul-making. For each minute of time is given to us to say "Aye" or "Nay" to our eternal destiny. Every now and then, there bursts in upon the mind a brief light from another world, revealing the precipice that stands before one, as well as the pull of the stars. Sometimes it is darkness that gives vision scope, but even to the most neglecting souls there comes that still, quiet voice of conscience beckoning one on to peace. It is an unsolicited favor and one procured at an infinite price, but it offers deliverance, peace to people of business fretted with anxiety, to parents with the care and delight of children, to youth in the full bloom and blossom of springtime promise, to the aged that the greatest life is yet beyond. This is a special kind of peace; it is above the human; it is also free. That is why it is called "grace." For a people to be living in a plague and refuse the antidote that could cure would be foolish. But how often it is true: "I would, but thou wouldst not." The greatest things in life are free, and greatest among these is divine Life — if we but seek it.

[GUIDE TO CONTENTMENT]

Unless souls are saved, nothing is saved; there can be no world peace unless there is soul peace. World wars are only projections of the conflicts waged inside the souls of human beings, for nothing happens in the external world that has not first happened within a soul.

[PEACE OF SOUL]

The Hymn of Life

THE UNIVERSE REVEALS the profound truth that all things, from the grain of sand on even to the angels, are singing a beautiful hymn of life to the Creator. This hymn has many verses, each one more beautiful than the preceding, and all leading up to a climax in man in the natural order and to Christ in the supernatural. All life reveals itself as a process of unification. To make unity out of multiplicity; homogeneity out of heterogeneity; the same out of the different; the permanent out of the passing — that is the fundamental movement of life.

This world would be like a gigantic puzzle-picture if there were no unifying force to put the pieces together. A mosaic is unintelligible if it is seen only in its details, but it takes on a new beauty when seen in its unity. The Mosque of Omar in Jerusalem has the magnificent beauty of its tinted windows ruined by the folly of petty lines running in crazy fashion about the walls. They lead nowhere; they are like blind leaders of the blind — there is nothing to unify them. Life is beautiful only when it is reduced to unity. . . .

* * *

The universe is a great sacrament. A sacrament in the strict sense of the term is a material sign used as a means of conferring grace, and is instituted by Christ. In the broad sense of the term everything in the world is a sacrament inasmuch as it is a material thing used as a means of spiritual sanctification. Everything is and should be a stepping-stone to God: Sunsets should be the means of reminding us of God's beauty, as a snowflake should remind us of God's purity. Flowers, birds, beasts, men, women, children, beauty, love, truth — all these earthly possessions are not an end in themselves, they are only means to an end. The temporal world is a nursery to the eternal world, and the mansions of this earth a figure of God's heavenly mansions. The world is just a scaffolding up which souls climb to the Kingdom of Heaven, and when the last soul shall have climbed through that scaffolding, then it shall be torn down and burnt with fervent fire, not because it is base, but simply because it has done its work.

A human being, therefore, partly works out his or her salvation by *sacramentalizing the universe;* we sin by refusing to sacramentalize it, or, in other words, by using creatures as selfish ends rather than God-ward means. Manichaeism is wrong because it considers matter as an evil instead of a "sacrament." Epicureanism is wrong because it considers pleasures as a God, instead of a means to God. Sacramentalizing the universe ennobles the universe, for it bestows upon it a kind of transparency that permits the vision of the spiritual behind the material. Poets are masters in sacramentalizing creation, for they never take anything in its mere material expression; for them things are symbols of the divine. Saints surpass poets in that gift, for saints see God in everything, or better, see God through everything. . . .

* * *

Why should a human being be bound to the office of holding commerce with God? Why should not a human being be independent of God? Humans could not be independent of God any more than a ray of sunlight could be independent of the sun. The absolute independence of the ray would mean its destruction, for it is only by being dependent on the sun that it survives. So it is with us in our relation with God. Let us make this clear by an example. If I should invent some great machine that would not only shorten human labor but add great material benefit to humankind, the government would give me patent rights on that invention. The rights would entitle me to all returns on my invention and would protect me against illegal encroachments of others. Now, we are "God's invention." Since we are His invention, He has "rights" on us, which means that He is entitled to the service of our intellect and our will, and it is this service that constitutes the true perfection and liberty of human beings and the foundation of all religion. In other words, God is entitled to our worship for the same reason every author is entitled to a royalty on his book — it is his creation....

* * *

As all creation revolves about humankind, so too humankind revolves about Jesus Christ. We are the pivot about which the whole order of nature swings; Jesus Christ is the pivot about which all supernature swings. This is the point to which we must ever recur, for without Christ this world of ours loses its intelligibility and meaning.

* * *

For those whose eyes see no further than the first vision of the universe, all the trees of the forest bear only the burden of leaves; for those who are gifted with a deeper vision, all the other trees of the forest bear the burden of penitent thieves. When someone dies, for the earthly-minded, not even the leaves chant a requiem; when a person dies, for the heavenly-minded, even the earth yawns and gives up its dead.

Both outlooks point to a tree, for it is the tree that matters now as in the beginning, when the first humans balanced a fruit against a garden. *Qui in ligno vincebat, in ligno quoque vinceretur.* Man fell by a tree, it is fitting that he be redeemed by a tree, for a tree is the crux of the whole philosophy of the universe, and the crux is the Cross....

* * *

Life is not completely under our control. Each tick of the clock brings us closer to our end; "our hearts are but muffled drums beating a funeral march to the grave." "From hour to hour we ripe and ripe; from hour to hour we rot and rot." Even the very food we eat, while nourishing us, gradually corrodes and wears away the machinery of our body.

And while truth is a condition of our nature, it is almost like a phantom, for the more we study the less we know, or rather the less we think we know. Profound study opens up new vistas of learning, worlds quite beyond our own, worlds of grace, each with laws of its own. How often, too, a search after truth corrects the prejudices of youth; how often earnest seekers after the Logos have come to mock and remained to pray. Great minds have confessed that after a life dedicated to the quest for truth, they felt that they were merely standing on its shores, while its great expanse stretched out infinitely before them. Thomas Aquinas, the greatest mind of Christian times, declared at the end of his life that all he had written was a straw compared to a vision that divine truth had accorded him.

[THE LIFE OF ALL LIVING]

Truth does not mean going out to the cosmos. It means the cosmos coming into the mind. Truth is not the heavens by themselves, but rather the heavens in the head, which is the primary condition of truth.

[OLD ERRORS AND NEW LABELS]

The Death of Life

G RACE IS no mere theological abstraction void of meaning and usefulness. Grace is life — the life of God among us. It is not something that cuts an unexpected tangent across the harmony of the universe, but rather it is that which perfects the universe in its highest earthly expression, viz.: humanity.

A treatise on grace might be called a Supernatural Biology, for the laws of organic life are feeble reflections of the laws of the life of grace. The very notion of biogenesis, the law that all life must come from previous life, and can never be spontaneously generated, is a natural truth that should prepare the mind for the supernatural truth that human life can never generate divine life, but that divine life must be a gift. Only life can give life, and only Life can come from Life. *Omne vivum ex vivo* is as true of supernatural biogenesis as it is of the natural. The life of God that is grace is a pure gift of God to which we have no right whatever. It was given to us in the first Adam, and restored to us by the merits of the second Adam, Jesus Christ.

The whole order of creation affords us an analogy of the gift-quality of grace. If a stone, say the Rock of Gibraltar, should suddenly break out into bloom, it would be something transcending its nature. If a rose one day would become conscious, and see and feel and touch, it would be a supranatural act — an act totally undue to the nature of the rose as such. If an animal would break out into a reasoning process and speak words of wisdom, it would be a supranatural act, for it is not in the nature of an animal to be rational. So too but in a far more rigorous manner, if a human, who by nature is a creature of God, becomes a child of God and a member of the family of the Trinity, and a brother or sister of Jesus Christ, it is a supernatural act for the human, and a gift that surpasses all the exigencies and powers of human nature, even more than blooming surpasses the nature and powers of marble.

Grace makes a person more than a "new creature," and infinitely higher than his former condition, than an animal would be if it spoke with the wisdom of Socrates. The difference between mere human life and human life rendered deiform by grace is not one of development, but of generation. The source of life in both cases is as different as human and divine parenthood. The distance that separates some minerals from the vegetable kingdom may be only a hair's breadth — but the distance that separates human life and divine life is infinite. "No one can pass from thence hence."

The least gift of grace, the great Thomas Aquinas tells us, is worth more than all created things. All the gold and precious stones; all the mansions of earth, and all its passing joys; the power of navies; the beauty of cities; the might of nature's harmonious forces; all these are as sounding brass and tinkling cymbals compared to the worth of grace infused into a soul at the moment of its incorporation into Christ. Meetings in Downing Street, conferences at the White House, League meetings at Geneva, and sessions at the d'Orsay, all these are but of ephemeral importance in an ephemeral world, compared to the meeting of the soul and Christ at the well of baptism....

"That which is born of the flesh, is flesh; that which is born of the Spirit, is spirit" (Jn 3:6). Being born of the flesh incorporates us into the life of Adam; being born of the spirit incorporates us into the life of Christ. The children of God are twice born; the sons of men once born. The true Renaissance is in the children of God who are reborn, not by entering again into their mothers' wombs, "for the flesh profiteth nothing," but by being born of God, becoming thereby His children and His heirs.

The children of God are in virtue of their relationship to God heirs of heaven; they pass into their heritage at death. The sons of men are heirs only of riches that rust consumes, moths eat, and thieves break through and steal. The children of God have within themselves the seed of glory and eternal happiness, but not so with the children of men. There is more difference between two souls on this earth, one in the state of grace, and the other not in that state, than there is between two souls, one in the state of grace in this life, and the other enjoying the eternal blessedness of heaven. The reason is that grace is the germ of glory and some day will blossom into glory just as the acorn some day will become the oak. But the soul not possessed with grace has no such potencies in it. "Dearly beloved," says St. John, "we are now the sons [and daughters] of God; and it hath not yet appeared what we shall be. We know that when He shall appear, we shall be like unto Him; because we shall see Him as He is" (1 Jn 3:2).

One wonders why a world so much given to the philosophy of evolution does not see the grace of Jesus Christ as the answer to its aspirations. One of the reasons why evolution is held so highly is the promise it gives for the future; and yet, all that it can give, even in its wildest form, is the unfolding of something beneath us. But here in supernatural biology, there is the promise and the potency of a glory for us that exceeds even our imagination — the potency not of becoming a superman, but a child of God. There is no emergent in the whole field of evolution comparable to the "new creatures" that emerge from the sacrament of Baptism. True greatness of life is not a push from below, but a gift from above: "I am come that you may have life and that in abundance" (Jn 10:10).

When we say there is a progress in life in living by the life of God, we do not mean that any human naturally or by his own powers is capable of meriting that life in strict justice, or growing into it as naturally as the acorn becomes the oak. Grace and glory in heaven are related as the acorn and the oak, but not the natural and the supernatural. It is absolutely impossible for a creature to share in the divine life of his own power. The analogy offered, which points out the gradual progression observed in created things from a lower to a higher nature, is merely a persuasion that our elevation is neither unreasonable nor untenable by a scientific mind, but it does not offer a proof of such elevation. We cannot agree that because chemicals and vegetables merge into a higher life, therefore humans do also; we can only suggest that if God does elevate humans to a participation in the divine life, He in no way destroys human nature but perfects it. The greater can never come from the lesser, and this applies not only to the supernatural, but to the natural order.

Life, in the broadest terms, continues to live as long as the higher order dominates a lower order, and when the soul lives by Christ Who is eternal, it too lives eternally. We are immortal in the natural order because God never forgot that He made us; we are immortal from the supernatural point of view because we live by the Immortal Christ.

Death is just the inverse of this, and it may be defined as the domination of a lower order over a higher order. The plant dies when the chemical order dominates it; a poisonous gas may kill the plant immediately, or else the slow wearing away of its tissues through the absorption of the chemical kingdom brings its death. An animal dies when a lower order, either the chemical or the vegetable, dominates it, either singly or in combination. Generally it is the slow oxidization of the organism that brings about its death. A human body dies in much the same way. The very food that we eat, and the air that we breathe, carry not only life with them, but death as well. The waste products of the food gradually poison the system and the very act of nutrition burns away the organs and the tissues slowly and surely, until finally they succumb and waste away.

But a human being has not only a body but also a soul. Both body and soul have their life; the life of the body is the soul and the life of the soul is Christ. Now when does the soul die? It dies when a lower order dominates it. And what is this lower order? It is the body. When body dominates the soul; when matter dominates the spirit; when that which is base dominates what is lofty; when that which is vicious dominates that which is virtuous; when the lower dominates the higher; then the soul dies, and it is here in the moral order that death is called *sin.* That is why the Sacred Scriptures use indifferently the terms "sin" and "death." "For, the wisdom of the flesh is death." "The wages of sin is death" (Rom 6:23). A person, therefore, may be living while he or she is dead; such a person may be alive physically but dead spiritually. And it is this idea of the higher life of God that was in the mind of the Apostle when he spoke of those who call themselves living but really are dead.

Imagine the funeral service of a person who lived in sacramental and mystic union with Christ throughout his life. His body is dead beyond all doubt, but his soul lives, not only with natural immortality, which it possesses, but with the very life of God. Suppose a pallbearer standing nearby is in the state of sin. In the eyes of God there is more death in the pallbearer than in the corpse; it is the pallbearer who really is dead and, if we were spiritually minded, we would weep over him and chant a requiem over his soul rather than over the departed one. The real death is not the death of the body, but the death of the soul.

[THE LIFE OF ALL LIVING]

Peace of soul comes to those who have the right kind of anxiety about attaining perfect happiness, which is God. A soul has anxiety because its final and eternal state is not yet decided; it is still and always at the crossroads of life. This fundamental anxiety cannot be cured by a surrender to passions and instincts; the basic cause of our anxiety is a restlessness within time that comes because we are made for eternity.

If there were anywhere on earth a resting place other than God, we may be very sure that the human soul in its long history would have found it before this.

[PEACE OF SOUL]

The Depths of Simplicity

T HE WORLD has one supreme test for character, and that is the possession of a virtue in a high and eminent degree. Many generals, for example, in our national history are ranked as great characters because of their valor, and many scientists are ranked as great characters because of their wisdom. Some are judged noble because of their love of peace, others because of their bravery in war; some because of their majesty, and others because of their gentleness; some because of their wisdom, others because of their simplicity.

But this is not the real way to judge character. The possession of one virtue in an eminent degree no more makes a great person than one wing makes a bird. Just as the eagle's power is measured by the distance from the extremity of one wing to the extremity of the other, so a person's character is to be judged, not by the possession of one extreme virtue but by the expanse between that virtue and the opposite one, which complements it. Character is nothing more nor less than the reconciling of opposite virtues. In other words, a really great character is not just a brave person, for if a person was brave without being tender, he or she might very easily become cruel. Tenderness is what might be called the other wing to bravery. In like manner, majesty alone does not make character, for majesty without gentleness might very soon degenerate into pride. Love of peace alone does not make character, for without the opposite virtue of courage, peacefulness could very easily slip into a spineless cowardice. Wisdom without simplicity makes a person proud; simplicity without wisdom makes a person a simpleton.

A real character, therefore, does not possess a virtue on a given point on the circumference without at the same time possessing the complementary virtue, which is diametrically opposed to it; for what is character but the tension between opposites, the equilibrium between extremes. Thus St. Paul exhibits in his life the beautiful tension between zeal and gentleness; St. John the tension between overflowing love and uncompromising devotion to truth; and Moses the tension between firmness and meekness.

Just as every engine must have its fly-wheel, every springtime its harvest, every ocean its ebb and its tide, so every really great character must have its pendulum so delicately adjusted that it can swing between the extremes of the magnanimous and the humble, the lofty and the plain, without ever once being detached. Character, then, is the balanced tension between opposite virtues.

It is in this sense that the character of Our Blessed Lord rises above all people and is the perfect exemplar of goodness and the paragon of virtues. One might show how He combined majesty and gentleness, peacefulness and force, magnanimity and humility, but for the sake of brevity we limit ourselves only to the two extreme virtues that the Lord recommended to His apostles at the beginning of His public life: wisdom and simplicity: "Be ye therefore wise as serpents and simple as doves" (Mt 10:16).

Our Blessed Lord did not make this recommendation without possessing it in an eminent degree Himself. He was wise with the Wisdom of God; but He was simple with the simplicity of a child. That is why He came to us as the world's God-Child. But what is more remarkable still, He never used His wisdom before the simple, but only before those who thought themselves wise. He was wisdom before the so-called wise, but He was simplicity before the simple. He exceeded the worldly wise with His wisdom and the simple with His simplicity.

He outdid the worldly wise with His wisdom. Take, for example, the scene in the temple at the beginning of His public ministry. The Pasch was drawing near, and pilgrims from Galilee began to gather into Jerusalem. Our Lord came with the throng and entered through the Golden Gate into the temple. As He passed beneath the arch and came into the Court of the Gentiles, the open space before the steps that led up to the Holy Place, a busy scene lay before Him. It was more than the mere jostling of crowds paying their yearly tribute of half a shekel to the temple treasury. Rather, here was a bedlam of confusion. In the heat of that April day were hundreds of merchants and shopkeepers mingling the cry of their wares with the bleating of sheep and the bellowing of oxen. There were little men with big wicker cages filled with doves, and under the very shadow of the arcades sat the money-changers wrangling in the most dishonest of trades, their greedy eyes aflame with the lust of gain. Everywhere there was huckstering, quarreling, bargaining, and the clanking of money to be heard above the chants of the Levites and the prayers of the priests. And all this at the entrance to the Temple of the Most High.

When Our Blessed Lord entered, a righteous indignation laid hold of Him, for what is character but a beautiful tension between force and meekness. An anger divorced from meekness is but unsanctified passion, and meekness that cannot kindle into indignation is closely allied to moral collapse. And on the occasion, Our Lord's swift indignation was just as much a part of His perfect sanctity as His silent meekness in the hour of the Passion. He could not, being justice itself, be silent before an offense against God. His eyes burned with a controlled anger; His firm face set in commanding scorn. His hands reached to some bits of binding cord lying on the floor beside Him. With His fingers, rapidly yet calmly, He knotted them into a whip. The traffickers stood still; the merchants eyed Him with growing fear; then they stepped back from Him as One Whom they had reason to fear.

Then quietly but firmly He began to move His tiny whip of knotted cord. The frightened crowd yielded, and sheep and cattle broke and fled. With His foot He overthrew the tables of the money-changers, as they rushed to the floor to gather up their jangling coins from the filth and pollution. Before those who sold doves He stood still, for the dove was the offering of the poor, and there was less desecration in their lovely emblems of innocence and purity. To these He was more gentle. He did not scatter them; He did not break the baskets and release the doves; to their owners He spoke tenderly: "Take these things hence, and make not the house of my Father a house of traffic" (Jn 2:16).

And His disciples, seeing this transport of inspiring and glorious anger, recalled to mind what David had written of Him in prophecy: "The zeal of thy house hath eaten me up" (Jn 2:17; Ps 69:9).

And if we ask why the greedy traffickers did not resist as their oxen were chased into the street and their money flung on the floor, the answer is because sin is weakness; because there is nothing in the world so utterly abject and helpless as a guilty conscience; because nothing is so invincible as the sweeping tide of God-like indignation against all that is base or wrong; because Vice cannot stand for a moment before Virtue's uplifted arm. Base and low as they were, every one of them who had a remnant of his soul not yet eaten away by infidelity and avarice knew that the Son of Man was right.

All the while there was standing on the marble steps that led up to the Holy of Holies a group of Levites, Scribes, and Pharisees who knew what a heavy loss that stampede would cause the merchants and themselves. They looked for the cause of the commotion and saw that He Who provoked it all was a carpenter from lowly Nazareth, with no mark of office about Him, no scrolls, no ensigns of dignity, but only an uplifted hand. They were indignant. How dare this obscure working man with a few ill-smelling fishermen as companions arrogate authority to Himself within the temple precincts, in which they alone were masters? They moved down the steps to Him, as He stood alone with the whip cord in His hand and asked Him: "What sign can you show us for doing this?" (Jn 2:18).

He might have pointed His finger at the panic-stricken crowd as a sign that all men fear the justice of God. But these were learned men, skilled in the Scriptures, and wise in their own conceits. And before those who thought themselves wise, Our Blessed Lord was wiser. He would show to them a wisdom so deep, so profound, so revealing the truth of their Scripture, that not even they, the wise men of Israel, would understand. In fact, what He said was so deep that it took them almost three years to understand it. Firmly and solemnly with a gesture centered on Himself, He said something beyond their comprehension, something that in its apparent meaning filled them with perfect stupor and angry amazement because they understood not its depth. The words were over their heads, at the same time they stole into their hearts: "Destroy this Temple, and in three days I will raise it up." . . .

Such wisdom was too profound even for the wise of this earth. It was not until almost three years later that it began to dawn upon them, when the Temple they destroyed on Good Friday was rebuilt by the power of God on Easter Sunday; and even the Truth too is so deep and profound that some of our wise men today have not yet begun to understand it even after nineteen hundred years.

[THE ETERNAL GALILEAN]

Grace and Faith in Christian Life

WHAT DOES THE SOUL feel like when it begins to encounter the grace of God?

1. The soul feels itself in a crisis. On the one hand, there is a profound sense of one's own helplessness and, on the other hand, an equally certain conviction that God alone can supply what the individual lacks. If there were *only* a sense of helplessness, there would be despair, pessimism, and eventual suicide. This is, indeed, the condition of the post-Christian pagan: He or she feels the total inadequacy of his or her own inner resources against the overwhelming odds of a cruel universe and thus falls into despair. Such a person has one-half the necessary condition for conversion — namely, a sense crisis — but he fails to link up his powerlessness with the divine power, Who sustains and nourishes the soul. But when this is done, paganism vanishes and gives place to what might be called creative despair: "despair," because one realizes one's own spiritual disease; "creative," because one knows that only a divine physician outside oneself can bring healing to one's wings. This despair does not usually arise from a sense of one's stupidity or ignorance or mistakes, but because of one's inadequacy, one's sense of dependence, or even one's admission of guilt.

2. The soul becomes the battlefield of a civil war during a conversion. It is not enough that there be a conflict between consciousness and unconsciousness or self and environment, for such tensions can be simply psychological. The tension or conflict is never very acute when the dueling forces are contained within the mind itself; conversion is not autosuggestion, but a flash of lightning from without. There is a great tension only when the self is confronted with the non-self, when the within is challenged by the without, when the helplessness of the ego is confronted with the adequacy of the divine.

Not until the tug-of-war begins, with the soul on one end of the rope and God on the other, does true duality appear as the condition of conversion. There must be in the soul the conviction that one is in the grip of and swayed by a higher control than one's own will; that, opposing the ego, there is a Presence before Whom one feels happy in doing good and before Whom one shrinks away for having done evil. It is relatively unimportant whether this crisis, which results in a feeling of duality, is sudden or gradual. What matters is the struggle between the soul and God, with the all-powerful God never destroying human freedom. This is the greatest drama of existence.

3. There is an impression that one is being sought by someone — by the "Hound of Heaven" in Thompson's language — who will not leave us alone. The tragedy is that many souls, feeling this anxiety, seek to have it explained away, instead of following it to where, at the end of the trail, it is seen as God and actual grace working on the soul. The voice of God causes discontent within the soul in order that the soul may search further and be saved. It embarrasses the soul, for it shows us the truth, tears off all the masks and masquerades of hypocrisy. But it consoles the soul too by effecting a harmony with self, with others, and with God. It is for everyone to decide — to accept or reject the voice he hears. Once these two currents of inner frustration and divine mercy meet, so that the soul realizes that God alone can provide what it lacks, then the crisis reaches a point where a decision must be made. In this sense, the crisis is crucial — it involves a cross. The crisis itself can take a thousand different forms, varying from souls that

are good to those that are sinful. But in both these extremes there is a common recognition that the conflicts and frustrations cannot be overcome by one's own energy. The common forms of crisis are the moral, the spiritual, and the physical.

4. The soul now wants to get out of its sins.

Up to this point, the soul had covered up its sins; now it discovers them in order to repudiate them. What is owned can be disowned; what is perceived as an obstacle can now be surmounted. The crisis reaches its peak when the soul becomes less interested in stirring up external revolutions and more interested in the internal revolution of its own spirit; when it swings swords, not outward but inward, to cut out its baser passions; when it complains less about the lying of the world and begins to work on making itself somewhat less a liar than before. The moral sphere has two ethical poles: one, the immanent sense of evil or failure; the other, the transcendent power of God's mercy. The abyss of powerlessness cries out to the abyss of salvation, for *copiosa apud eum redemptio*. The Cross is now seen in a new light. At one moment, it bespeaks the depth of human iniquity that, in essence, would slay God; at another moment it reveals the defeat of evil in its strongest moment, vanquished not only by the prayers for forgiveness from the Cross but by the triumph of the Resurrection.

But this cascade of divine power cannot operate on those who live under the illusion either that they are angels or that sin is not their fault. A person must first admit the fact of personal guilt; then — though the consciousness of having been a sinner does not vanish — the consciousness of being in a state of sin is relieved. This is probably the experience to which Charles Péguy referred when he said, "I am a sinner, a good sinner."

Once the will to sin is abandoned, then the soul sees that it has become acceptable to the Savior — not because it was good, but because the Savior is good. The moral crisis is ended when Christ confronts the soul, not as law but as mercy, and when the soul accepts the invitation, "Come to me, all you that labor, and are burdened, and I will refresh you" (Mt 11:28).

5. There is a definite change in behavior and conduct of life. Not only does conversion change one's values; it also reverses the tendencies and energies of life, directing them to another end. If the convert before conversion was already leading a good moral life, there is now less emphasis on keeping a law and more emphasis on maintaining a relationship of love. If the convert has been a sinner, his spiritual life frees him from habits and excesses that before weighed down the soul. He often finds that these practices were not so much appetites as attempts to flee responsibility or to ensure, by plunging into unconsciousness, that he could avoid the necessity of choice. Before conversion, it was behavior that to a large extent determined belief; after conversion, it is belief that determines behavior. There is no longer a tendency to find scapegoats to blame for the faults of self, but rather a consciousness that the reformation of the world must begin with the reformation of self. There is still a fear of God, but it is not the servile fear a subject has for a dictator, but a filial fear, such as a loving child has for a good father or mother whom he would never wish to hurt. From such a Love one does not ever need to run away, and the previous acts of dissipation, which were disguised forms of flight, are now renounced.

Once the soul has turned to God, there is no longer a struggle to give up these habits; they are not so much defeated as crowded out by new interests. There is no longer a need of escape — for one is no longer in flight from oneself. Having done one's own will, such a one now seeks to do God's will; he who once served sin now hates it; she who once found thoughts of God dry or even unpleasant now hopes above all else one day to behold the God Whom she loves. The transition the soul has undergone is as unmistakable as the passage from death to life; there has been, not a mere giving up of sin, but such a surrender to divine love as makes one shrink from sin because one would not wound the Divine Beloved.

6. The soul also receives *certitude*. Philosophy gives a proof for the existence of God; the science of apologetics gives the motives for believing in Christ, the Son of God; but all the incontrovertible proofs

they offer fall short of the certitude that actually comes to a convert through the gift of faith. Imagine a young man whose father has been lost for years. A friend, returned from a trip, assures him that he has certain evidence that his father really exists on another continent. But the young man is not fully satisfied with the evidence, however convincing it is; until he is restored to his father's actual presence, he will not have peace. So it is with conversion: Before, one knows *about* God; afterward, one *knows* God. The first knowledge the mind has is notional and abstract; the second is real, concrete, and it becomes bound up with all one's sentiments, emotions, passions, and habits. Before conversion, the truths seemed true but far off; they did not touch one personally. After conversion, they become so personalized that the mind knows that it is through with the search for a place to live; it can now settle down to the making of a home. The convert's certitude is so great that his mind does not feel that *an* answer has been given, but *the* answer — the absolute, final solution, which one would die for rather than surrender.

Those who have never gone through the experience of a complete conversion imagine that reason must be completely abdicated for such a step. We hear them make such remarks as, "I cannot understand it; he seemed like an intelligent man." But those who have gone through the experience of conversion see that just as the eye winks, closing itself to the light for an instant that it may reopen and see better, so too one winks his reason for that brief instant in which he admits that it may not know *all* the answers. Then, when faith comes, the reason is found to be intact and clearer-sighted than before. Both reason and faith are now seen as deriving from God Himself; they can never, therefore, be in opposition. Knowing this, the convert loses all doubts. His certitude in his faith becomes unshakable — indeed, it is his old notions that are now apt to be shaken by the earthquake of his faith.

7. Another effect is: *peace of soul.* There is a world of difference between peace of mind and peace of soul. Peace of mind is the result of bringing *some* ordering principle to bear on discordant human experiences; this may be achieved by tolerance, or by a gritting of one's teeth

in the face of pain; by killing conscience, or denying guilt, or by finding new loves to assuage old griefs.

The peaceful soul does not seek, now, to live morally, but to live for God; morality is only a by-product of the union with God. This peace unites the soul with his neighbor, prompting one to visit the sick, to feed the hungry, and to bury the dead.

All the energy that was previously wasted in conflict — either in trying to find the purpose of life or in trying alone and futilely to conquer one's vices — can now be released to serve a single purpose. Regret, remorse, fears, and the anxieties that flowed from sin now completely vanish in repentance. The convert no longer regrets what he might have been; the Holy Spirit fills his soul with a constant presentiment of what he can become through grace. But since grace rejuvenates, it quickens even the old to consecrated service.

And there are many other ways in which peace of soul will manifest itself after conversion: It makes somebodies out of nobodies by giving them a service of divine sonship and daughtership; it roots out anger, resentments, and hate by overcoming sin; it gives the convert faith in other people, who are now seen as potential children of God; it improves one's health by curing the ills that sprang from a disordered, unhappy, and restless mind; for trials and difficulties, it gives one the aid of divine power; it brings one at all times a sense of harmony with the universe; it sublimates one's passions; it makes one fret less about the spiritual shortcomings of the world because he or she is engrossed in seeking personal spiritualization; it enables the soul to live in a constant consciousness of God's presence, as the earth, in its flight about the sun, carries its own atmosphere with it. In business, in the home, in household duties, in the factory, all actions are done in the sight of God, all thoughts revolve about God's truths. The unreasonable blame, the false accusations, the jealousies and bitterness of others, are borne patiently, as Our Lord bore them, so that love might reign and that God might be glorified in the bitter as in the sweet. Dependence on God becomes strength; one no longer fears to undertake good works, knowing God will supply the means.

But above all else, with this deep sense of peace, there is the gift of perseverance, which inspires us never to let down our guard, or to shrink from difficulties, or to be depressed as the soul presses on to its supernal vocation.

[GO TO HEAVEN]

How long the conflict between good and evil will last we do not know; how long we will walk down the road bemoaning persecutions and crucifixions before God makes His presence known to us we do not know; how long we will seek the living among the dead, as did Magdalene, we do not know; how long we will crouch in fear behind closed doors before the Light of the World breaks through with "Peace be unto you," we do not know.

There is only one thing we do know, and that is that we have already won — only the news has not yet leaked out!

[CROSS-WAYS]

The First Faint Summons
to Heaven

W E CANNOT keep God out; God has His own way of getting into the soul. There are two breaches in our walls;
two cracks in our armor; two hidden entrances to the
soul through which God can enter. These are so much a part of our
nature that we cannot alter them. When God made us, He built them,
like trap doors, in our natures. Even when our intellects bar God's
passage by the false obstructions to belief that unsound thinking has
erected, He is able to penetrate to us through the secret doors we have
not known how to bolt.

The first of these trap doors in the soul is the love of goodness. As
we chase after every isolated tidbit that attracts us by its good, the soul
is really in pursuit of the whole and infinite goodness of God. Every
quest of pleasure, every love of a friend, every approval of a good child,
every comparison of good and better, implies some goodness beyond all
these good things, for none of them completely fills our hearts. Every
lesser good we approve intimates our longing for utter goodness, for
God. To say that we want good things but not goodness, which is God-
ness, is like saying that we love the sunbeams but we hate the sun, or
we like the moonlight but despise the moon. The substance of the sun
does not reach our room with the sunbeam, but some participation of
it does; and, in like manner, no part of God is in the good apple, the

good friend, but a participation of that goodness is always there. No one can love the good without implicitly loving goodness, and to that extent God creeps into the soul in its every wish and every joy.

Because of this human predilection for what is good, no life is made up entirely of actions that are intrinsically wicked. The murderer savors the true goodness of a good dinner; a thief responds to the virtue of a child; a gangster feeds soup to poor people out of honest generosity. Good deeds are mingled with evil deeds. No one is forever persecuting, sinning, blaspheming; sometimes a hardened sinner is engaged in planting a rose, nursing a sick friend, fixing a neighbor's tire.

There are considerable hidden reserves of natural goodness in everyone; they live on stubbornly in company with one's predominant passion, even if that is turned toward evil. Because there is something in us that escapes infection, we are never intrinsically wicked, never incurable, never "impossible." Those who see our good deeds admire us; and those who see only our bad deeds hold us low. That is why there can be such divergent judgment about someone. Even when the will is perverse — even when a creature is enthralled and captivated by one great sinful adhesion, which makes one's days a flight from God toward lust or power — even then there are some few good and commendable acts that contradict one's general attitude. These isolated acts of virtue are like a clean handle on a dirty bucket; with them, God can lift a soul to His peace.

The second trap door by which God enters a soul in flight from Him is by its ennui, its boredom, its satiety, its fed-up-ness, its loneliness, its melancholy, its despair. No matter how many evils we may have chosen, we have never exhausted the possibilities of choice — the human is still free; his power of choice is never exhausted. Every libido, every passion, every craving of the body, is finite, and the body's cravings, when satisfied, fail to content us. But in the life of the weary sensualist, there is still one choice that has never been made, one great chord that has not yet been struck. He has not tried the infinite. Statements like "I have seen life" and "I have tried everything" are never true, because the people who speak this way have not explored the greatest adventure of all. The rich person still asks: "What do I yet lack to make me happy?" The rich one knows, as all sensation seekers know, that gratifying every whim still leaves the deepest appetites unsatisfied. There is always still something to be had — something we need badly. We know, but we do not know everything; we love, but not forever. We eat, and we still hunger; we drink, and we still thirst: "The eye is not filled with seeing, neither is the ear filled with hearing" (Eccl 1:8).

Despite our efforts to find contentment in the temporal, we fail. For as the fish needs the water and the eye needs light, as the bird needs air and the grass needs earth, so the spiritual soul needs an infinite God. Because God, for Whom we were made, is left out of its reckoning, the soul feels an emptiness, a boredom with what it has, a yearning for what it has not. This ennui is the negative presence of God in the soul — just as sickness is the negative presence of health in the body, and hunger is the negative presence of food in the stomach; a lack in us points to the existence of something capable of filling it. Through this trap door of our emptiness, God enters. If we do not admit God at first, God will intensify the dissatisfaction and the loneliness, until finally He is accepted as our soul's guest and its eternal host.

[Go to Heaven]

The holy hour in our modern rat race is necessary for authentic prayer. Our world is one of speed in which intensity of movement is a substitute for lack of purpose; where noise is invoked to drown out the whisperings of conscience; where talk, talk, talk gives the impression that we are doing something when really we are not; where activity kills self-knowledge won by contemplation. . . .

There seems to be so little in common between our involvement with the news of the world and the Stranger in whose Presence we find ourselves. The hour means giving up a golf game or a cocktail party, or a nap. . . .

Sometimes it is hard, especially during vacation when we have nothing to do. I remember once having two hours between trains in Paris. I went to the Church of Saint Roch to make my holy hour. There are not ten days a year I can sleep in the daytime. This was one. I was so tired, I sat down at 2:00 P.M. — too tired to kneel — and went to sleep. I slept perfectly until 3:00 P.M. I said to the Good Lord: "Did I make a holy hour?" The answer came back: "Yes! That's the way the Apostles made their first one." The best time to make a holy hour is in the morning, early, before the day sets traps for us. By being faithful to it, and letting nothing interfere with it, we use it as the sign and symbol of our victimhood. We are not called to great penances, and many would interfere with our duty, but the hour is our daily sacrifice in union with Christ.

[THOSE MYSTERIOUS PRIESTS]

The Training of Children

I N THE ORDER OF NATURE, not many things are capable of being trained. Water, for example, is capable of assuming only three different forms: vapor, ice, and liquid. Crystals have their shapes rigorously determined by the law of nature. In the animal kingdom, it is very dubious whether fleas can be trained, though elephants and dogs can. No one ever says to a little pig, "What kind of hog are you going to be when you grow up?' But one does ask a child, "What kind of person are you going to be?"

Children are either trained by us toward a fixed goal and destiny, or they are trained in spite of us. The parents never have the alternative of deciding whether their child's mind will be full or empty. It cannot be kept empty; it will be filled with something. Passions, television, movies, streets, radio, comic books — all of these contrive against a perpetual vacancy in the mind of the child. Like a little octopus's, his arms are reaching out either for food or for poison.

The great tragedy today is that parents themselves are so often without any convincing standards to offer for the guidance of their children. They have the sextant but no axed star, the technique but no destiny, the material but no blueprints, the means but no ends. When Picasso gives us part of a face, a twisted limb divided by a broken world, surmounted by a geometrical figure, we are staring at the tragedy of our times — a broken personality no longer resembling the Divine Image.

Rudyard Kipling once said, "Give me the first six years of a child's life; you can have the rest." Napoleon was once asked, "When does the education of a child begin?" He answered, "Twenty years before its birth — in the education of its mother."

In order properly to train the child, parents must be mindful of its three basic instincts:

1. The instinct for eternity

2. The instinct for love

3. The instinct for the Divine

1. *The instinct for eternity.* It is difficult for children to conceive things otherwise than they actually are. There would have to be certain experiences of life in order to perceive change. Since young children are at the beginning of life, they are unable to understand such things as age and death and birth. For the moment they are voyagers without baggage. They live in the present and imagine it to be eternal. That is why when the mother leaves the house, the child will invariably cry, because to the child the mother is leaving the house forever. Dogs probably look very sad for exactly the same reason. They, too, know less the succession of time, but live in a permanence that is akin to eternity.

Because they live in the eternal, children's imagination is infinite. Beanstalks do actually climb to the sky; they mount a broomstick and imagine themselves mounted on a great beast, "clinging to the whistling mane of every wind." Superman, Captain Midnight, and other characters who fly from one planet to another are very real and alive in the infinite universe of the child. Bathing in ease in the great miracle of creation, the child only later on becomes impressed with a transition that underlies all creation.

Associated with this instinct of the infinite and the eternal is the child's love of truth. No child is ever born a skeptic or an agnostic. Agnostics and skeptics are made not by thinking, but rather by behavior, that is, bad behavior. A child cannot understand a lie. Everything the father tells him is absolutely true. He may even justify a statement by saying that "it is in a book," never suspecting that lies could be printed as well as told.

Suppose the parents completely neglect to train the child in the infinite eternal truth, which he already knows by instinct. The child will then begin to live in a small universe, and nothing is so small as a materialistic universe, or a purely humanistic world in which there are only struggling, weak humans. If religious education is abandoned, as the child grows in age, the world in which he lives will become smaller and smaller until finally the only world that is left is his tiny little ego, in which he is imprisoned with his selfishness and ignorance — and he has to go to a psychiatrist to get him out.

Woe to the parents who contract by neglect the infinite yearnings of a young heart, and through failure to give them religious training prepare their children for nothing but stunted and warped lives! . . .

* * *

2. *The instinct of love.* Every child presumes love, and rightly so, for he soon learns that love was waiting for him when he came into the world. Mother's love preceded him in the sense that her body was a kind of a living ciborium in which he was housed as a host. The air, food, shelter, sun, and stars were all there with their little tokens of love; all the resources of earth gathered about the cradle, offering themselves. The father perhaps already had his cigars bought, and perhaps a bicycle in anticipation that it would be a boy. The cradle, the layette, the toys — all were marks of love that preceded and existed before him. The child comes to them, but he does not create them. Love is something like life; we cannot create it; we can only communicate it. Fire cannot be taken from the coal unless a blaze or a fire is brought to the coal. Love, however, comes from without.

Later on, when the child becomes conscious, he retains his capacity for love. His first question returning from play is: "Where is Mother?" in order that he may tell her something that has happened. Mother must listen to all of the incidents in his life. The father must identify

himself with his games, his sorrows, and his joys. The child then comes
to see that the eye has vision, but the light was there first; the ear can
hear, but the sound was there first; the brain is there, but is surrounded
by an outer world; the will is there, but goodness envelops it; the intellect is there, but so is truth as its environment. As trees in the forest
nudge and push their branches against other trees in order to discover
the light, so the child pushes and nudges his way to bathe in the love
that preceded him.

Suppose now the parents fail in this love. One of the effects is that
children may grow up to hate because they are hated. A little girl is
teased by her older brother. The older brother may like the Brooklyn
Dodgers. Because she now bears some enmity toward her older brother,
she develops a fondness for the Yankees, not because she likes the Yankees, but because she does not like her older brother. Where there is no
environment of love, there is hate. Children whose parents are quarreling may grow up to be those who hate marriage, hate society, and
hate law.

The parents, however, who understand the meaning of love will say
to their children, "Love existed before you were born. You found love
waiting for you. Now we want you to know, because you are older, that
our love is nothing but a reflex of God's love. We are mirrors reflecting
back the love that we received. As our love preceded you, so God's
love preceded us. God loved us first. We do not want you to rest in the
rays of our love; we want you, through these rays, to go back again to
the source of love. We do not want you to content yourself with merely
the sparks of human love that you find here in the family hearth; we
want you to think about the Flame of Love that is God. You will grow
into a world where there is bitterness, hate, suspicion, selfishness, and
ingratitude. When you find people who are not lovable, you must realize that all of them are loved by God. If you do not have the love
of God on which to repose when others cut and tear your heart, your
life will be sad and disillusioned. As you had many blessings in this
house, because you breathed the atmosphere of love, so you will have
many blessings in life if you put yourself in the area of God's love. As

a homeless waif is denied many blessings such as food, clothing, and shelter because he is outside of the environment of love, so your life will be without great happiness, if it is outside of that Great Love that came to this earth and said, 'Love one another as I have loved you.'"

3. *The instinct for the Divine.* Every child endows his father with two attributes: omnipotence and omniscience. His father can do all things, and his father knows all things. The father to the child is God, and he worships him in secret. He is stronger than any other man in the world, and he knows more than any other father in the world. He is different from all other fathers. The child likes the way he walks, the way he wear his clothes, the way he smokes, and the way he comes into the house from work. The father, therefore, takes God's place in the home and reveals, whether the child knows it or not, the justice of God. In that identification with the father is the child's self-esteem, his pride, and his glory: "The Father and I are one." In that sense, the Christhood of the child seeks to do all things that are pleasing to him.

The mother to the child is the incarnation of gentleness, meekness, forgiveness, understanding. The mother finds excuses for his failure, tempers the severity of a father's justice, discovers extenuating circumstances that put him outside of a too severe reprimand. The mother is the court of equity in the home; the father is the court of law. The mother reveals that other attribute of divinity — which is mercy, love, and forgiveness. When the mother threatens, "I will tell your father," the child will often beg her to keep secret his failure, that he may enjoy her mercy.

To every child, parents are the mirrors of perfection; the father is the strongest, the mother is the nicest. The two images in some way confound and reveal the sovereign justice and the merciful goodness of God.

The greatest shock of youth is disillusionment with the parents. The child may become disillusioned about the father when there is a quarrel with his mother, or when he hears the father swear, or tell a dirty story, or come home late. There is a bewildering and a personal humiliation on discovering that his father is just like any other father and his mother is just like any other mother. The fall of the idol threatens his whole being. This disenchantment, depression, and emptiness will be with the child through life, unless the parents have fortified themselves with the true concept of the Divine, which they now pass on to their children. In that case, the parents can say, "We are the imperfect image of divine justice and divine mercy. Once you understand the justice of God, you will go through life with a sense of law, right, duty, and honor; once you have a sense of the mercy of God, then in the midst of your falls and your sins there will not be a denial of guilt, but a throwing of yourself into the arms of One Who died to save your soul." Without this concept of the justice and the mercy of God, the child may become sulky and aggressive and moody. With it, a love of his parents will deepen, and he will be prepared to become a parent.

It is no wonder Our Blessed Lord reminded us that we would enter the Kingdom of Heaven only on condition that we become as little children. The special attributes of the children that He recommended are humility, unworldliness, simplicity, teachableness, which are the direct contraries of self-seeking worldliness, distrust, and conceit. The child is a model because he bathes himself in eternity, in love, and in a sense of the Divine.

Turning around the statement of the Savior, Our Blessed Lord was saying that no old people will ever enter the Kingdom of Heaven — old in the sense of being wise in their own conceits. I shall look for you in the nurseries of heaven.

[Love, Marriage and Children]

What Are You Like?

TAKE YOUR HEART into your hand as a kind of crucible and distil out of it its inmost nature. What do you find it to be? Are you not really a bundle of contradictions? Is there not a disparity between what you *ought* to do, and what you actually do? Do you not sometimes feel like a radio tuned into two separate stations, heaven and hell, getting neither but only static and confusion worse confounded?

The Latin poet Ovid expressed your sentiments perfectly when he said: "I see and approve the better things of life, the worse things of life I follow." St. Paul, too, expressed your inmost moods when he cried out: "I do not do the good I want, but the evil I do not want I do" (Rom 7:19).

You feel dual, divided against yourself because you more often choose what you like, rather than what is best for you. When you do, you always feel the worse for it. Somehow, within you there is a "kink"; your human nature is disorganized. You feel frustrated; your realizations are anticlimaxes; they turn out to be the opposite of what you expected. You are a problem to yourself, not because of your more obvious faults but because the better part of you so often goes wrong.

Your soul is the battlefield of a great civil war. The law of your members is fighting against the law of your mind. Your name is "legion" — you have no unifying purpose in life; there is only a succession of choices, but there is no one overall goal to which everything is subordinated. You are split into many worlds: eyes, ears, heart, body, and soul. In your more honest moments you cry out:

> *"Within my earthly temple there's a crowd:*
> *There's one of us that's humble, one that's proud;*
> *There's one that's broken-hearted for his sins*
> *And one who unrepentant sits and grins;*
> *There's one who loves his neighbor as himself,*
> *And one who cares for naught but fame and self.*
> *From much corroding care I should be free,*
> *If once I could determine which is me."*
>
> From *A Little Brother of the Rich, and Other Verse,*
> by Edward Sanford Martin

How explain this basic contradiction within you? There are four false explanations: psychological, biological, intellectual, and economic.

The psychological explanation attributes this tension within you to something peculiar to you as an individual, to your erotic impulses, for example, because you were frightened by a mouse in a dark closet during a thunderstorm while reading a book on sex.

This hardly fits the facts because you are not the only one who is "that way"; everyone is. There is nothing odd about *you*. But there is something odd about *human nature*. Do not think that basically you are any different from anyone else in the world, or that you have a monopoly on temptations, or that you alone find it hard to be good, or that you alone suffer remorse when you do evil. It is human nature that is odd, not you.

The second false explanation is biological: The kink in your nature is due to a fall in evolution.

No! *Evil is not due to the animal in you.* Your human nature is very different from the animal's. There is a great discontinuity between a beast and a human. As Chesterton says: "You never have to dig very deep to find the record of a man drawing a picture of a monkey, but no one has yet dug deep enough to find the record of a monkey drawing the picture of a man."

An animal cannot sin because it cannot rebel against its nature. It *must* follow it. We can sin because we merely *ought* to follow our nature. When you see a monkey acting crazily in a zoo, throwing banana peels at spectators, you never say: "Don't be a nut." When, however, you see a person acting unreasonably, you say: "Don't be a monkey." Man alone can be subhuman; he can sink to the level of a beast.

The peculiar thing about human beings is that, though we may cease to act like a human being, we never lose the imprint of human dignity. The divine image with which we were stamped is never destroyed; it is merely defaced. Such is the essence of human tragedy. We did not evolve from the beast; we devolved to the beast. We did not rise from the animal; we *fell* to the animal. That is why unless the soul is saved, nothing is saved. Evil in us presupposes what it defaces. As we never can be godless without God, so we never could be inhuman without being human.

The third false explanation attributes the evil in you to want of education: You are perverse because you are ignorant. Once you are educated, you will be good.

No! You do not have this inner contradiction because you lack knowledge, for the educated are not all saints and the ignorant are not all devils. Enlightenment does not necessarily make you better. Never before in the history of the world was there so much education, and never before was there so little coming to the knowledge of the truth. Much of modern education is merely a rationalization of evil. It makes clever devils instead of stupid devils. The world is not in a muddle because of stupidity of the intellect, but because of perversity of the will. We know enough: It is our choices that are wrong.

Finally, the socialist explanation of this tension, namely, that people are wicked because they are poor, does not explain the facts.

Never before were living standards so high. All the rich are not virtuous, and all the poor are not wicked. If you had all the money in the world, you would still have that bias toward evil. If poverty were the cause of evil, why is it that juvenile delinquency increases in periods of prosperity, and why does religion prosper in the vow of poverty? If poverty were the cause of evil, then riches should be the source of virtue. If that is so, why are not the wealthy the paragons of virtue?

The world has not just made a few mistakes in bookkeeping that any expert accountant or economic advisor can correct; rather the world has swindled the treasury of faith and morality. It is not the world's arithmetic that is incorrect; it is our morals that are bad.

Since this perversion of human nature is universal, i.e., since it affects human nature (not just your personality exclusively or mine), it must be due to something that happened to human nature itself at its very origin.

Second, since it is not animal in its origin, but has all the earmarks of being deliberate and the result of a free choice, it must not be a part of God's original work, but must have come into being through some tendency to evil.

Third, since evil is not merely a by-product of bad environment but is endemic in the human heart, it cannot be explained except on the basis of a universal fracture of some great moral law to which we are all bound.

Some acts of disobedience can be remedied. If I throw a stone through a window, I can put in a new window. But there are other kinds of disobedience that are irremediable, e.g., drinking poison. Since evil is so universal in the world, it must be due to a disobedience of the second kind and thus affects us in our inmost nature.

Either God created you the way you are now, or else you are fallen from the state in which God created you. The facts support the second view: The present tension and inner contradiction within are due to some fault subsequent to the creation of human nature....

* * *

The fact remains: Whatever you are, you are not what you ought to be. You are not a depraved criminal, but you are weak; you are not a mass of irremediable corruption, for you bear within yourself the image of God. You are like a person fallen into a well. You know you ought not to be there, and you know you cannot get out by yourself.

This is a roundabout way of saying that you need religion, but not a religion with pious platitudes. You want healing; you want deliverance; you want liberation. You know very well that there are a thousand things in your life that you thank God have not been found out by others. You want to get rid of these things. You do not want a religion to cheer you up on the roadway of life regardless of which road you take.

Analyzing your soul, you discover it to be like an auto that has run out of gas, and you are not quite sure of the right road. Hence, you need someone not only to give you some fuel for your tank, but also someone to point out your destination. If you have no religion at the present time, it may be because you rightly reacted against those bland assumptions that a few moral exhortations on Sunday will transform the world into the Kingdom of God.

You want a religion that starts not with how good you are, but with how confused you are.

* * *

You can love the lovable without being religious; you can respect those who respect you without religion; you can pay debts without being religious, but you cannot love those who hate you without being religious; you cannot atone for your guilty conscience without being religious.

Possibly the only reason in the world for loving the unlovely, for forgiving the enemy, is that God is love; and since as such He loves me who am so little deserving of His love, I also ought to love those who hate me.

* * *

The true view of human nature lies somewhere in between two extremes: absolute goodness and total depravity — between optimism and pessimism. Your experience tells you that you are not a saint, but it also tells you that you are not a devil. The tendency toward evil in you is not an irremediable flaw, but an accident that can be controlled.

You feel like a fish on top of the Empire State Building; somehow or other you are outside of your environment. You cannot swim back, but Someone could put you back. You feel yourself like a clock that has all the works and still will not "go," because you have broken a mainspring. You cannot supply the new mainspring. The original Watchmaker could supply it. Somewhere along the line, human nature became bungled, and it has all the earmarks of having been upset by a false use of freedom.

When you buy an automobile, the manufacturer gives you a set of instructions: the pressure to which you ought to inflate your tires; the kind of oil you ought to use; and the proper fuel to put in the gas tank. He has nothing against you by giving you these instructions, as God had nothing against you in giving you commandments. The manufacturer wants to be helpful; he is anxious that you get the maximum utility out of the car. And God is anxious that we get the maximum happiness out of life. Such is the purpose of His commandments.

We are free. We can do as we please. We *ought* to use gas in the tank, but if we please, we can put in Chanel No. 5. Now there is no doubt that it is nicer for our nostrils to fill the tank with perfume rather than with gasoline, but the car simply will not run on Chanel No. 5. In like manner, we were made to run on the fuel of God's love and commandments, and we simply will not run on anything else. We just bog down.

[PREFACE TO RELIGION]

Teen-Agers

ADOLESCENCE, or "teen-age," is the short hour between the springtime and the summer of life. Before the teen-age is reached, there is very little individuality or personality, but as soon as the teens begin, the emotional life takes on the character of its environment, like water takes its shape from the vessel into which it is poured. The adolescent begins to be conscious of himself and others, and for that reason begins to live in solitude. The youth is more lonely than many parents and teachers know; perhaps the teen-ager agonizes in a greater solitariness of spirit than at any other time in life until maturity, when the sense of unrequited guilt begins to weigh down the human soul.

As the teen-ager projects his or her personality to the world about, he seems to get further away from it. Between the teen's soul and the world there seems to be a wall. There is never a complete self-analysis. As it takes an infant a long time to coordinate its eyes and its hands, so it takes the teen-ager a long time to adjust completely to this great broad world to which he feels so strangely related. The teen-ager cannot yet take it in stride; novelty, new emotional experiences, great dreams, and hopes flood the teen's soul, each demanding attention and satisfaction. Teens do not confide their emotional states to others; they just live. It is hard for the adult to penetrate the shell into which the teen-ager crawls. Like Adam after his fall, the teen hides from discovery.

Along with this loneliness, there goes a great desire to be noticed, for egotism is a vice that has to be mastered early in youth. This craving for attention accounts for the loudness in manner of some teen-agers. Not only does it attract the gaze of others, but it also reflects a latent sense of rebellion against others and affirms that the teen is living for himself in his own way or as she pleases.

Along with this quality of inpenetrability the teen-ager becomes an imitator almost like the Japanese. Being in rebellion against the fixed, and being governed largely by fleeting impressions, the teen becomes like a chameleon, which takes on the colors of the objects upon which it is placed. He becomes a hero or a bandit, a saint or a thief, depending on the environment or his reading or his companions. This spirit of imitation reveals itself in the style of dress, haircuts, etc. All these become universal among youths who are afraid to march "against the grain."

There are few natural leaders among teen-agers, most of them being content to follow others. In this unconscious mimicry of others is a moral danger, for character is dependent on the ability to say "No." Unless education can give to teen-agers a training of the will, many of them will slip into adulthood and become slaves of propaganda and public opinion the rest of their lives. Instead of creating, they imitate. To create is to recognize the spirit in things; to imitate is to submerge personality at the lowest level of the mass.

Elders must not be too critical of the teen-agers, particularly when teens rebel against them. From one point of view they are not in rebellion against restraint, but against their elders for not giving them a goal and purpose of life. The teen-ager's protest is not conscious. Teens do not know why they hate their parents, why they rebel against authority, why their friends are becoming more and more delinquent. But the real reason is under the surface; it is an unconscious protest against a society that has not given the teen a pattern of life. The schools the teen attends have seldom stressed restraint, discipline, or self-control. Many of the teachers have defined freedom and even democracy as the right to do whatever you please. When this temporary phase of rebellion is past, the teen-agers will look for some great cause to which they can make a total dedication. They must have an ideal. In many instances today, they have no greater object of worship than to wrap their emotional lives around a sports figure, a movie star, a band leader, or a singer. This sign of decaying civilizations will pass when the catastrophe comes. Then youth will look for a different type to imitate, namely, heroes or saints.

A sad commentary it is on our civilization that the teen-agers have never rallied around our war heroes. This is because they are not yet ready for the more solid ideal. But it will come. And when it does, education must be careful lest in reacting against "progressive" education devoid of discipline, teens follow false sacrificial gods. The latent capacity for doing the brave and heroic that is in every youth will soon come to the surface, and when it does, please God, it will be both for heroes and saints that they center their affection.

The ascetic ideal has passed away from the elders, but God sends fresh generations into the world to give the world a fresh start. Our teen-agers will one day find their right ideals, in love of country and love of God, and particularly the latter, for it is the function of religion to make possible to everyone sacrifices that in the face of reason or egotism would never come to the surface.

[Way to Happiness]

More About Teen-Agers

THE PSYCHOLOGY of teen-agers is as important as it is interesting. The dominant characteristics are: interiority, imitation, and restlessness.

1. *Interiority.* A trait often missed because of the energy of youth is its consciousness of solitude and its sense of aloofness born of the realization that a kind of barrier is thrown up between itself and the world. Boys try sometimes to overcome this barrier by shaving before their time, thus leaping the wall between adolescence and manhood; girls affect it in dress or other mannerisms in order to bridge the gap. Gestures are clumsy, uneasy, ungraceful; arms seem too long and always in the way; words have little value for exchange purposes with adults in establishing contact with the grown world. There are more images than ideas in the interior world, which may account in part for the inability to establish rapport with others. Sometimes this very ineptitude increases interiority and drives the youth back into himself or herself.

Because exterior actions do not always give release to the inner world, the teen-ager often has recourse to an inner world of images where he or she has an interior adventure, picturing himself as a hero on a football field, or herself as married to a prince. Movies are popular because they are a good feeder for such daydreams and hopes. The general picture, however, is of one who has suddenly arrived at a growing interior depth but, not knowing its value, expresses himself or herself badly.

2. *Imitation.* There is a profound philosophical reason for imitation. The ego is under the imperative and need of emerging from itself as a chrysalis; the interior is bursting to affirm its personality. Imitation becomes a substitute for originality; originality commits the youth to effort, labor, pain, perseverance, and sometimes the scorn of others; but imitation gives one the needed exteriorization through a kind of social conformism. Locked up in itself, youth must emerge. Since it is harder to be oneself, and at that age one does not quite know what is oneself, it becomes a hero-worshipper; hence the fan clubs, fanaticism for players of percussion instruments, the idolizing of some so-called movie star.

That is why in the high school age one finds very few who ever dress outside of the pattern set by a few. The creative minority in adult life is also few; therefore the youth must not be taken to task for imitation. This mimicry could be dangerous if what was idolized were low; but it can be also one of the ennobling influences of youth if those who are imitated are noble, good, and patriotic. Youth imitates because it wants to create, and creation marks the end of interiority in a constructive way.

3. *Restlessness.* Perhaps a better description of restlessness would be a mercurial affection. There is extreme mobility in youth, due to the multitude of impressions that flood the soul. Life is multiple; there is little harmony because of the great variety of appeals from the external world. Hence the appeal to certain youths of a certain type of music; it provides an outlet for sense energy that has not yet been rationalized. Because of this agitation, it is difficult for a youth to fix his or her attention on any one object; perseverance in study is hard; the impulsions of the moment solicit with a loud voice. This could end in delinquency if the activity never found a target.

But at the same time, like the other characteristics, it can also be the salvation of the youth, for they are really running around the circumference of human experience in order to decide on which particular segment they will settle for life; they tour the world of professions, avocations, and positions and then decide in which they will repose. Once this energy becomes canalized, focused, and rationalized, it becomes the beginning of a life's work, and an adolescent begins to be what God intended — a person who in loving virtue knows how to love others.

[WAY TO HAPPINESS]

In moments of crisis and doubt, in worries whether to undertake this task or omit it, to go on this journey or not, listen to the voice of the Spirit within. The union of your soul and the Holy Spirit can become a kind of spiritual marriage, giving the joys of the spirit born of a unity that leaves all other joys as sorrows, and all other beauty as pain. For the first time in your life, you would begin to love not that which is lovely, but that which is Love: the Spirit of the Most High God.

*   *   *

Do not fear God, for perfect love casts out fear. God is biased in your favor. Would you rather be judged by the justice of the peace of your town on the last day, or by the King of Peace? Most certainly by God, would you not? David even chose a punishment at God's hands rather than man's, for he knew God would be more lenient.

God is more lenient than you because He is perfectly good and, therefore, loves you more. Be bold enough, then, to believe that God is on your side, even when you forget to be on His. Live your life, then, not by law, but by love. As St. Augustine put it: "Love God and then do whatever you please." If you love God, you will never do anything to hurt God, and, therefore, never make yourself unhappy.

[PREFACE TO RELIGION]

Content with
Sawdust Brains?

I F ONE CAME into a city a perfect stranger and saw people hilarious, gay, and happy, exchanging gifts and greetings with one another, and abounding in good cheer, but with no apparent reason for such happiness, one would wonder if they were out of their heads.

Once a year, at Christmas time, everyone is happy and loving, kind and generous. But one wonders if they know why they are happy. The reason for the joy and happiness of Christmas we will explain with dolls — but before doing so, a word about what Christmas has done to time, space, and the Missing Link.

Christmas did something to time. Everyone is born in a certain era of time over which he or she has no control. But when Eternity came to this earth and established His beachhead in Bethlehem, time was struck with such a terrific impact that it was split in two. From that moment on, all the periods of history have been divided into the period before Christ (B.C.) and the period after Christ (A.D.), *Anno Domini*, the year of the Lord.

Not only was time split in two, but space was turned upside down. The Greeks believed that their gods dwelt on Olympian heights. This worried them to some extent, because if God is "way up there," what does He know about our sufferings? They wanted a God Who was in the dust of human lives. What did a God in the heights know about being a refugee, about being homeless? Was He ever betrayed? Did He ever suffer? Did He ever come close to death? But when the Son of God was born under the floor of the world in Bethlehem, He shook the world to its very foundations. More than that, He turned space upside down. Until then, mothers always used to say, as they held children in their arms, "Heaven is way, way up there"; but the day that the Woman held the Babe in her arms, it began to be true to say that she "looked down" to heaven.

Finally, Christmas is the discovery of the Missing Link. During the last one hundred years scholars have been concerned about finding the human's relationship to the beast. Distressingly enough during that same period of time, humans have almost acted like beasts. Christmas is the discovery of the Missing Link — not the link that binds us to the beasts, but the link that binds us to God. The divine Babe was the real Cave Man, for He was born in a cave of Bethlehem. The light that is shining in His eyes is not that of a beast coming to the dawn of reason, but the light of God coming to the darkness of humanity; His name is not Piltdown, but Christ. Being God and Man, He is the link between both. Life is now discovered to be not a push from below, but a gift from above.

Now we come to the explanation of Christmas. Remember the song the doll sang after having been repaired, and how she wondered if the little girl would love her after she got back from the doll hospital?

> I'm a little doll who was dropped and broken
> Falling off my mommy's knees;
> I'm a little doll who has just been mended;
> Now, won't you tell me please
> Are my ears on straight?
> Is my nose in place?
> Have I got a cute expression on my face?
> Are my blue eyes bright?
> Do I look all right to be taken home Christmas day?

When I first came here just a month ago
Brought in by a little girl who loved me so,
She began to cry 'til they told her
I could be taken home Christmas day.

Christmas time is drawing nearer and I'm getting scared;
Wish I could see in a mirror how I've been repaired.
I'll be called for soon but I've worried so;
Will she love me like she did a month ago?
Are my ears on straight?
I can hardly wait to be taken home Christmas day.

Christmas is the repairing of human nature or human dolls. . . .

* * *

Christmas is not something that has happened; it is something that is happening. The real problem is something like that of the doll, though we change the words to read, "Is my heart on straight? Is my soul in place? Do I have a love expression on my face? Is my soul full of God's light? Do I look all right to be taken to the crib on Christmas morn?"

[Life Is Worth Living]

"Nice" People

THIS SUBJECT can be introduced by the story of the egotist who went to see a physician, complaining of a headache. The doctor, upon examination, asked, "Do you feel a distressing pain in the forehead?" "Yes," said the patient. "And a rather throbbing pain in the back of the head?" "Yes." "And piercing pains here at the side?" "Yes." The doctor explained: "Your halo is on too tight."

The point is that almost all people today believe that they have a halo. If it does not come from virtue, at least it comes from a shampoo. Mark Twain once said, "When I reflect upon the number of disagreeable people who I am told have gone to a better world, I am moved to lead a different life."

A distinction must be made between "nice" people and "awful" people.

The nice people *think* they are good; the awful people *know* they are not. The nice people never believe they do wrong, or break a commandment, or are guilty of any infraction of the moral law. If they do anything that reason would call wrong, they have various ways of explaining it away. Goodness is always their own, but badness is due to something outside themselves. Some say that it is due to economic circumstances: One will say, "I was born too rich" and another, "I was born too poor." Psychology also comes in handy to explain away their faults, for example, "I have an Oedipus complex" or an "Electra complex," or "I have an inferiority complex."

The awful people, on the contrary, generally are not rich enough to be psychoanalyzed; they have never been introduced to their subconscious, and they think themselves just plain bad. Nice people, if they are guilty of intemperance, will call themselves alcoholics. Awful people call themselves drunkards — sometimes just plain "bums." The nice people say they have a disease. The drunkards say, "I am a no-good." The nice people judge themselves by the vices from which they abstain; the awful people judge themselves by the virtues from which they have fallen. When a nice person sees another doing something that he regards as wrong, he criticizes; when an awful person sees a man going to death on a scaffold, he says with St. Philip Neri, "There go I but for the grace of God." When a nice person really sins, he says, "What a fool I am." When an awful person really sins, he says, "What a sinner I am."

The nice people always follow the ethics of social orthodoxy, or convention. They lose less sleep over falsifying an income-tax return than over wearing a white tie instead of a black one at a banquet, or are more scandalized at a preacher's grammatical errors than at his false doctrine. Refinement and respectability form a large concept in the nice person's goodness, and social convention is given the force of a divine command; what is respectable or usual is not wrong. Living in a society where divorces are common, the nice people say, "Well, everybody is doing it; therefore, divorce is right." The nice people think they are going straight because they are traveling in the best circles; the awful people are those whose vices are open and who are generally below the level of social convention. When nice people break all the commandments of God, their friends say that "she is so nice" or "he is so nice"; when the awful people break a few of the commandments in a grosser way, they are labeled "low and unrefined." Nice people love to read scandals about nasty people because it makes them feel so good. In truth, the nice people are those whose sins have not been found out; the awful people are those whose sins have been found out.

*   *   *

The nice people do not find God, because, denying personal guilt, they have no need of a Redeemer. The awful people, who are passionate, sensual, warped, lonely, weak, but who nevertheless make an attempt at goodness, are quick to realize that they need another help than their own; that they cannot lift themselves by their own bootstraps. Their sins create an emptiness. From that point on, like the woman taken in sin, it is "Christ or nothing."

What surprises there will be on the Last Day when the awful people are found in the Kingdom of Heaven: "The harlots and the publicans will enter the Kingdom of Heaven before the Scribes and the Pharisees" (Mt 21:31). The surprises will be threefold. First, because we are going to see a number of people there whom we never expected to see. Of some of them will we say, "How did he get here? Glory be to God, look at her!" The second surprise will be not seeing a number of the nice people whom we expected to see. But these surprises will be mild compared with the third and greatest surprise of all, and that surprise will be that we are there.

[LIFE IS WORTH LIVING]

Love Begins
with a Dream

THERE *had* to be some such creature as Mary — otherwise God would have found no one in whom He could fittingly have taken His human origin. An honest politician seeking civic reforms looks about for honest assistants. The Son of God beginning a new creation searched for some of that goodness that existed before sin took over. There would have been, in some minds, a doubt about the power of God if He had not shown a special favor to the woman who was to be His Mother. Certainly what God gave to Eve, He would not refuse to His own mother.

Suppose that God in making over man did not also make over woman into a new Eve. What a howl of protest would have gone up! Christianity would have been denounced, as are all male religions. Women would then have searched for a female religion! It would have been argued that woman was always the slave of man and even God intended her to be such, since He refused to make the new Eve, as He made the new Adam.

Had there been no Immaculate Conception, then Christ would have been said to be less beautiful, for He would have taken His Body from one who was not humanly perfect! There ought to be an infinite separation between God and sin, but there would not have been if there was not one woman who could crush the cobra's head.

If you were an artist, would you allow someone to prepare your canvas with daubs? Then why should God be expected to act differently, when He prepares to unite to Himself a human nature like ours, in all things save sin?

But having lifted up one woman by preserving her from sin, and then having her freely ratify that gift at the Annunciation, God gave hope to our disturbed, neurotic, *gauche*, and weak humanity. Oh, yes! He is our model, but He is also the Person of God! There ought to be, on the human level, someone who would give humans hope, someone who could lead us to Christ, *Someone who would mediate between us and Christ as He mediates between us and the Father.* One look at her, and we know that a human who is not good can become better; one prayer to her, and we know that, because she is without sin, we can become less sinful.

[THE WORLD'S FIRST LOVE]

Emergence of Character

EVERYONE IN THE WORLD is defeated in one area of life or another. Some fall away from their high ideals; others bemoan their failure to marry or, having married, lament because the state failed to realize all its hopes and promises; others experience a decline of virtue, a gradual slipping away into mediocrity, or a slavery to vice; others are subjected to weariness, a failure of health, or economic ruin. All these disappointments are voiced in the mournful regret: "If I only had my life to live over again!" But it is of the utmost importance that, in facing our defeats and failures, we shall never yield to discouragement; for discouragement, from a spiritual point of view, is the result of wounded self-love and is therefore a form of pride. . . .

* * *

We can actually defeat defeat — use our failures as assets and our sins as stepping-stones to sanctity. This Christian attitude stands in sharp contrast to the methods of education. Education takes hold of what is best in a person, e.g., a talent for music, a gift for invention, or a taste for literature and develops that, to the exclusion of the arts and sciences for which we have no bent. And this is proper — we do not want our sculptors forced to specialize in law. A person's vocation is decided to a great extent by his or her capabilities.

But character training, on the contrary, takes as deep an interest in a person's greatest lacks as in his greatest gifts. It singles out his predominant failing and, by fighting against it, finally perfects the personality in the virtue contrary to the previous vice.

The first step in character training, then, is to discover what is worst in us. This is done by an examination of the sin to which we are most frequently tempted. It is very wrong to think that, because we are tempted, we are wicked. Sacred Scripture tells us: "My brothers and sisters, when you ever face trials of any kind, consider it nothing but joy, because you know that the testing of your faith produces endurance" (Jas 1:2). The blessedness of temptation is twofold. It reveals the weak spot in our character, showing us where to be on guard; and the same temptation gives us an occasion for gaining merit by refusing to submit to it.

Self-examination reveals the basic defect in each person's character, what is known as one's predominant fault. The predominant fault is the one that prevails over all other faults and to some extent inspires our attitude, judgments, and sympathies. Every individual temperament, despite its variegated expressions, generally follows one consistent line. It makes little difference that the hidden evil may be in the most remote corner of the heart; it may have been covered from others' sight, but the mind cannot help being aware that it is there. No spiritual progress can be made until the master fault is dug up from its hiding place, brought into the light, and laid before God. For until the position of the enemy is known, he cannot be attacked.

The secret of character training is to strengthen this weak spot in our character in cooperation with God's grace. The evil must be called by its right name when it is discovered; otherwise we shall excuse our lack of fortitude as an "inferiority complex" and our inordinate love of the flesh as a "release of the libido." Judas missed salvation because he never called his avarice by its right name — he disguised it as love of the poor.

Considerable probing is necessary to drag out the predominant fault; it always fights against being recognized. Sometimes it can be detected by discovering what defect makes us most angry when we are accused of it: The traitor flies into a rage when he is first accused of being disloyal to his country. The sin we most loudly and vehemently condemn in others may be the sin to which our own heart is most addicted: Judas, again, accused Our Lord Himself of not loving the poor enough. As Aristotle wisely remarked: "Every man judges of what is good according to the goodness or badness of his interior disposition." If we confront the world with the idea that everyone is dishonest, it is amazing how often that initial bias will be confirmed. This is because, just as water seeks its own level, so does the mind seek the level of its prejudice. Thieves consort with thieves, drunkards with drunkards, the prejudiced with the prejudiced.

The predominant fault is discoverable not only in the environment it keeps, or in the atmosphere it breathes, but also in the way that others act toward us. Nature acts as it is acted upon; be suspicious of a neighbor, and the neighbor acts suspiciously. Show love to others, and everyone seems lovable. The law of physics that every action has a contrary and equal reaction has its psychological counterpart. If we sow the seed of distrust in society, society always returns the harvest of distrust. The emotional reprisals of others can be used as the mirror of our own interior dispositions.

Once one has discovered the primary fault through any of these methods, the next step is to combat the interior defect. This requires a daily, even hourly struggle; sanctification is not a *place* at which one arrives but a *way* one travels. There are generally four ways of overcoming the predominant fault: (1) By asking God in prayer to illumine the dark places of the soul and to give us strength to conquer the sin. As the Council of Trent says: "God never commands the impossible; but in giving us His precepts, He commands us to do what we can, and to ask for the grace to accomplish what we cannot do." (2) By daily examination of conscience. Almost all people count the money in their pockets daily to determine whether the current expense of the day can be met; but how few of us ever balance our conscience to see if we are going into debt morally and spiritually. (3) By imposing on oneself a penance every time we succumb to the predominant fault, e.g., by saying a prayer for the absent person against whom we bore false judgment, or by giving five times the amount of a cock-tail to the poor every time we are tempted to intoxication by the first drink. (4) By making the predominant fault the occasion of a greater virtue.

This fourth method is one that is too often ignored, although strength of character cannot be had without a knowledge of our weakness and the ultimate mastery of it. "My grace is sufficient for you, for power is made perfect in weakness" (2 Cor 12:9). The storm reveals the weakness in the roof; but the part of it that was damaged and repaired is apt, later, to be the strongest. Scar tissue is the strongest skin of all. Kites and airplanes rise against the wind, not with it. Earth does not reveal its harvest without plowing, nor the minds their treasure without study, nor nature its secrets without investigation. One's defect, overcome, may become one's greatest strength.

Goodness is too often confused with passivity. There are a number of people who are considered to be good, when really they have not enough courage to do either a very good or a very evil act of any kind. But character does not depend on a want of energy to do wrong; it requires the use of great energy in doing right when wrong solicits us. The greatest sinners sometimes make the greatest saints: A Saul who hated became a Saul who loved; a sensuous Magdalene became a spiritual Magdalene. The convents and monasteries are full of potential devils — saintly souls who could have been very wicked men and women, in their vitality, if they had not corresponded to God's grace. Little St. Thérèse said that if she had not been responsive to God's mercies, she would have been one of the most evil women who ever lived.

On the other hand, the prisons of our country house a population of potential saints; the energy the criminals used in sinning was not wrong — it was the use to which they put their energy that was wrong. Lenin was probably a saint in reverse; if he had used his energy in violence toward self and the cultivation of love, instead of in violence toward others and the cultivation of hate, he could have become the St. Francis of the nineteenth century.

Some years ago, a young boy was badly burned in an explosion at his country school and was told he would never walk again. Instead of becoming discouraged, he concentrated on his infirmity, rubbed his legs, exercised them, then walked, and finally became one of the greatest mile runners in the history of America. This boy's power was made perfect in infirmity. Demosthenes not only stuttered in his youth, but he had a weak voice; he would never have become one of the world's greatest orators had he not worked to correct this weakness, transforming it into his greatest strength. Abraham Lincoln was defeated in almost every office for which he ran — until he was elected President of the United States. When Ludwig von Beethoven became deaf, he said, "What a sorrowful life I must lead"; then, rising above the first defeat, he said, "I will seize facts by the throat," and wrote great music he could never hear. When Milton went blind, he used his blindness itself as the inspiration for one of his finest poems.

Apply this valiant spirit to the spiritual life; here, too, the handicaps can be a spur. It is a basic fact that no saint ever found it easy to be good; to believe differently is the great mistake most people make in judging them. The law running through heaven and earth is that "in the case of an athlete, no one is crowned without competing according to the rules" (2 Tim 2:5). The Church never canonizes anyone unless he or she has shown a degree of holiness that is called heroic — and the virtues of the saints were the *opposites* of the natural weaknesses they had to overcome. The special quality of soul that might have made someone else a devil gave the saints their greatest opportunities for growth.

The moral quality always associated with Moses is meekness — but Moses was not born meek; he was probably hot-headed, quick-tempered, and irascible. For Moses killed an Egyptian — and that is not the mark of a meek person. He was also the first one to "break" the Ten Commandments; coming down from the Mount where he had conversed with God, he found his people adoring the Golden Calf and, in a fit of anger, smashed the Tablets of the Law. Anger is not meek; the weak spot in Moses was his hot-headedness. But this man turned the

worst in him into the best, so that later on — in his conduct toward the
fickleness of Pharaoh, in his attitude toward the ingratitude and way-
wardness of those whom he delivered, in his bearing toward his family,
in his final disappointment at not entering the Promised Land — he
maintained such an even temper that Sacred Scripture describes him
as "very humble [meek]" (Num 12:3). Moses acquired meekness by
fighting against an evil temper. He rooted out the worst in him; and
then, with God's help, he became one of the best of men.

In the New Testament, the character most often praised for charity is John; toward the end of his life, he preached incessantly on the
theme "Love one another." John describes himself as the "beloved dis-
ciple," and to him was given the privilege of leaning on the breast of
Our Divine Savior on the night of the Last Supper. But John was not
always so loving. He once tried to play politics through his mother,
getting her to ask Our Lord to give him and his brother the seats clos-
est to Our Lord when He came into His Kingdom. Charity does not
try to dominate or rule. On another occasion, when the city of the
Samaritans rejected Our Lord, John and his brother, James, asked Our
Lord to rain down fire from heaven to destroy the city. Charity is not
vengeance. There must, in truth, have been a tendency toward hatred
in John, for the Lord called him a Son of Thunder. But at some time
or other in John's life, he *seized* upon the weak spot in his character —
upon his want of kindness to his fellow man — and through cooperation with grace he became the greatest apostle of charity, the virtue he
had lacked before....

*   *   *

The temptations of the saints were seen as opportunities for self-
discovery. They allowed temptations to show them the breaches in the
fortress of their souls, which needed to be fortified until they would become the strongest points. This explains the curious fact about many
saintly people — that they often become the opposite of what they
once seemed to be. When we hear of the holiness of some souls, our
first reaction is: I knew him when...." Between the "then" and the
"now" has intervened a battle in which selfishness lost and faith won

out. They followed the advice of Paul: "[L]et us also lay aside every weight and the sin that clings closely" (Heb 12:1). They became what they were not.

Because the development of character requires constant vigilance, our occasional failures must not be mistaken for the desertion of God. Two attitudes are possible in sin — two attitudes can be taken toward our lapses into sin: We can fall down and get up; or we can fall down and stay there. The fact of having fallen once should not discourage us; because a child falls, it does not give up trying to walk. As sometimes the mother gives the most attention to the child who falls the most, so our failures can be used as a prayer that God be most attentive to us, because of our greater weaknesses. I always liked this incident in the life of St. Mary Magdalen de Pazzi. One day while dusting a small statue of Our Lord in the chapel, she dropped it on the floor. Picking it up unbroken, she kissed it, saying: "If you had not fallen, you would not have gotten that." Sometimes, in the case of a continued weakness, it is well to count not only the falls, but to count also the number of times a temptation to do wrong was overcome. The reverses we suffer in the heat of battle can lead us to strengthen our purposes.

The trials and temptations of life prove that in each individual there is an actual I-potential. The "actual ego" is what I am now, as a result of letting myself go. The "possible I" is what I can become through sacrifice and resistance to sin. Persons are like those ancient palimpsests or parchments, on which a second writing covered over the first; the original gloss of sin and selfishness has to be scraped off before we can be illuminated with the message of divinity.

No character or temperament is fixed. To say "I am what I am, and that I must always be," is to ignore freedom, divine action in the soul, and the reversibility of our lives to make them the opposite of what they are. In baptizing the duke of the Franks, the bishop reminded him of how he could reverse his past: "Bend your proud head, Sicambre; adore that which thou hast burned and burn that which thou hast adored." No character, regardless of the depths of its vice or its intemperance, is incapable of being transformed through the cooperation of divine and human action into its opposite, of being lifted to the I-level and then to the divine level. . . .

* * *

Character building, however, should not be based solely on the eradication of evil, for it should stress, even more, the cultivation of virtue. Mere asceticism without love of God is pride; it is possible to concentrate so hard on humiliating ourselves that we become proud of our humility, and to concentrate so intently on eradicating evil as to make our purity nothing but a condemnation of others. The difference in the two techniques — pulling up the weed or planting good seed — is illustrated in the ancient story of the Greeks: Ulysses, returning from the siege of Troy, wished to hear the Sirens, who sang in the sea, tempting many a sailor to his doom. Ulysses put wax in the ears of his sailors and strapped himself to the mast of the ship — so that even if he wished to answer the appeal of the Sirens he would be saved from doing so. Some years later, Orpheus, the divine musician, passed through the same sea; but he refused to plug up his sailors' ears or bind himself to a mast. Instead, he played his harp so beautifully that the song of the Sirens was drowned out. . . .

* * *

When a character is motivated by love alone, it finds much more goodness in the world than before. As the impure find the world impure, so those who love God find everyone lovable, as being either actual or potential children of God. This transformation of outlook takes place not only because love moves in an environment of love, but principally because, in the face of the love diffused by the saint, love is created in others. As jealousy in A begets jealousy in B, so generosity in A begets generosity in B. Love begets love; if we are kind, we get kindness back. The lover gets much more out of the world than the person who is cool or indifferent: He or she has not only the happiness of receiving, but the happiness of giving as well. Even when our love is not reciprocated by the wicked, the barbed word or the insult never hurts us. A priest once told St. John Vianney that a priest as ignorant of theology as he was should never go into a confessional box. The curé answered: "Oh, how I ought to love you, for you are one of the few who know me thoroughly. Help me to obtain the favor I have been seeking so long... to withdraw myself into a corner and to weep for my sins."

Love makes us loathe the faults that hold us back from love. But we are not disheartened over them — for our failings are never insurmountable, once they are discovered and recognized as such. It is excusing them or labeling them falsely that prevents our spiritual progress. Most important of the rules for attacking evil in ourselves is to avoid direct, in favor of indirect, assaults. Evil is not *driven* out — it is crowded out....

* * *

Sustaining all our efforts to develop character, there is a memory of the divine plea: "Come to me, all you that are weary and are carrying heavy burdens, and I will give you rest" (Mt 11:28). Not until a nobler, finer love is found can a person master his or her vices or overcome mediocrity. In a complete conversion, souls that were formerly addicted to vice no longer feel any desire for their old sins, but rather a disgust. As the eye blinks at dust, so the soul now blinks at evil. Sin is not fought; it is rather no longer wanted. Love casts out sin as well as fear. The great tragedy of life is that so many persons have no one to love. As a man in love with a noble woman will give up all that displeases her, so a soul in love with God gives up all that might wound that Love.

* * *

There is today far too much public discussion, analysis, and probing of evil, drunkenness, infidelity, illicit sex. It is as if the investigators reveled in uncovering sordid details. But the Church, in her understanding, demands that the details of our sins be excluded even from confession. Nothing so induces morbidity as concentration on the disease, while offering no cure except the patient's own homemade remedies, or those of an analyst, who silences suggestions when the fee stops. Relief from fundamental evil is never found on the human level, but on the divine. When Charles de Foucauld, a hero of France but an evil man, entered a church one day, he knocked at the confessional of Father Huvelin and said: "Come out, I want to talk to you about a problem." Father Huvelin answered: "No, come in; I want to talk to you about your sins." Foucauld, struck by divine grace, obeyed; later on he became a solitary in the desert and one of the most saintly individuals of our times....

*   *   *

Whoever is charged with character formation will do well to lay hold of what is best in people, searching for the gold and not the dross. There is something good in everybody. After the death of a street cleaner who had a reputation for dissolute living and infidelity and cruelty to his wife and children, most of his fellow street cleaners recalled all the evil about him except one companion who said: "Well, whatever you say about him, there was one thing he always did well. He swept clean around the corners." In dealing with ourselves, we should look for what is worst and make it, with God's grace, the occasion of spiritual growth. But in dealing with others, we should look for what is best, in order that, as we show mercy to others, God may show the grace of His mercy to us.

The right and the wrong methods of character formation are revealed in Our Lord's story of the unclean spirit:

"When the unclean spirit has gone out of a person, it wanders through wanderless regions looking for a resting place, but it finds none. Then it says, I will return to my own house from which I came. When it comes it finds it empty, swept, and put in order. Thereupon, it goes and brings along seven other spirits more evil than itself, and they enter and live there; and the last state of that person is worse than the first. So it will be also with this evil generation" (Mt 12:43–45).

Our Lord is telling us here that it is never enough to be free from the powers of evil; we must also be subject to the power of the good. The elimination of an ego does not necessarily imply the happiness of the I, unless the I, in its turn, lives by a higher spirit of love. The ego in the story has been rid of its evil occupant — it looks orderly and decent; it is swept and garnished. But it is empty, and an empty house decays more quickly than one that is occupied. So, when there is no ruling principle or master enthusiasm to take over the soul vacated of its ego, the emptiness can be preempted by some other force that is also evil.

There is a parallel to this in the political order, from which, a few centuries ago, ethics and morality and religion were exiled — only to find that, in the twentieth century, irreligion, atheism, and antimoral forces entered the political order to take their place. Casting out the unclean spirit is not enough, unless there is a new possession by a cleaner spirit. Nature abhors a vacuum. There is no such thing as a nonreligious individual; one is either religious or antireligious. Consciously or unconsciously, as time goes on, one's mind takes on some new allegiance; if God is lacking, that person becomes more and more captive to some temporal mood or fancy. Unless the new spirit of love comes in to take possession of the atheist, one of three other spirits will come to take charge — that of pride, or lust, or avarice.

No one is ever safe against the tyranny of the ego except through the power and love of God. The only way of keeping evil out is to let God in. Character building does not consist in the elimination of vice, but in the cultivation of virtue; not in the casting out of sin, but in the deepening of love. The person who wishes to expel evil without praying for the presence of God is doomed to failure. Nothing is secure until God is there and until God's Love is spread throughout our hearts....

* * *

Great patience is required to effect this transformation. If characters become impatient, it is because they fail to realize the great heights that have to be attained. Because the perfection at which we aim is lofty and difficult, human souls need and should gladly accept the calm, pure happiness the Infinite Designer sometimes sends them. We should not insist on constant strife against ourselves; there is a time for reaping in the spiritual life. Joylessness can hold us back from God.

A want of resoluteness, too, can spoil our efforts, for, as St. James says: "[T]he doubter being double-minded and unstable in every way, must not expect to receive anything from the Lord" (Jas 1:8). This halfhearted temper in character development sees prayer as something that may do good, and in any case can do no harm; it trusts in God, but it places a greater reliance on the economic solution for its ills. It first plans and prays, and then tries to perform the plan without the prayer. Character cannot develop under conditions of such disorder, confusion, and dividedness. Conflict of such a kind makes the mind tired, as it tries to blend two things that will not mix, fatigues itself in crossing from one road to the other.

Character is built by singleness of purpose, and nothing so unifies our goals as a temptation that is overcome, a conflict resolved by the love that not only shows the answer, but gives us the strength to reach for it. The search for spiritual unity is identical with the effort to perfect the character. And since there is no unity except in the truth that is God, the quality of our search will depend on where we place the emphasis in the sentence "I seek the truth." If the stress is put on the I, the character is ego-centered still, and truths are merely values to be assimilated for our vainglorious growth. But if it is the *Truth* toward which we wish to grow, our souls are able, at last, to disregard the self and overflow its narrow boundaries.

[LIFT UP YOUR HEART]

Prayer and Meditation

T HE ESSENCE OF PRAYER is not the effort to make God give us something — as this is not the basis of sound human friendships — but there is a legitimate prayer of petition. God has two kinds of gifts: First, there are those that He sends us whether we pray for them or not; and the second kind are those that are given on condition that we pray. The first gifts resemble those things that a child receives in a family — food, clothing, shelter, care, and watchfulness. These gifts come to every child, whether the child asks for them or not.

But there are other gifts, which are conditioned upon the desire of the child. A father may be eager to have a son go to college, but if the boy refuses to study or becomes a delinquent, the gift that the father intended for him can never be bestowed. It is not because the father has retracted his gift, but rather because the son has made the gift impossible. Of the first kind of gifts Our Blessed Lord spoke when He said: "He sends rain on the righteous and on the unrighteous" (Mt 5:45). He spoke of the second kind of gifts when He said: "Ask, and the gift will come."

Prayer, then, is not just informing God of our needs, for God already knows them. Rather, the purpose of prayer is to give God the opportunity to bestow the gifts He will give us when we are ready to accept them. It is not the eye that makes the light of the sun surround us; it is not the lung that makes the air envelop us. The light of the sun is there if we do not close our eyes to it, and the air is there for our lungs if we do not hold our breath. God's blessings are there — if we do not rebel against His will to give.

The person who thinks only of himself says only prayers of petition; the one who thinks of his neighbor says prayers of intercession; whoever thinks only of loving and serving God says prayers of abandonment to God's will, and this is the prayer of the saints. The price of this prayer is too high for most people, for it demands the displacement of our ego. Many souls want God to do *their* will; they bring their completed plans and ask God to rubber-stamp them without a change. The petition of the "Our Father" is changed by them to read: "My will be done on earth." It is very difficult for the eternal to give Himself to those who are interested only in the temporal. The soul who lives on the ego-level or the I-level and refuses to be brought to the divine level is like an egg that is kept forever in a place too cool for incubation, so that it is never called upon to live a life outside of the shell of its own incomplete development. Every I is still an embryo of what a person is meant to be.

Where there is love, there is thought about the one we love. "Where your treasure-house is, there your heart is too" (Mt 6:21). The degree of our devotion and love depend upon the value that we put upon a thing: St. Augustine says, *Amor pondus meum;* love is the law of gravitation. All things have their center. The schoolboy finds it hard to study, because he does not love knowledge as much as athletics. Business executives find it hard to think of heavenly pleasures because they are dedicated to the filling of their "barn." The carnal-minded find it difficult to love the spirit because their treasure lies in the flesh.

We become like that which we love: If one loves the material, one becomes like the material; if one loves the spiritual, one is converted into it in his outlook, his ideals, and his aspirations. Given this relationship between love and prayer, it is easy to understand why some souls say: "I have no time to pray." They really have not, because to them other duties are more pressing; other treasures more precious; other interests more exhilarating. As watches that are brought too close to a dynamo cease to keep time, so, too, hearts that become too much absorbed in external things soon lose their capacity to pray. But as a jeweler with a magnet can draw the magnetism out of the watch and reset it by the sky, so too it is possible to become de-egotized by prayer, and be reset to the eternal and to love divine.

A higher form of prayer than petition — and a potent remedy against the externalization of life — is meditation. Meditation is a little like a daydream or a reverie, but with two important differences: In meditation we do not think about the world or ourselves, but about God; and instead of using the imagination to build idle castles in Spain, we use the will to make resolutions that will draw us nearer to one of the Father's mansions. Meditation is a more advanced spiritual act than "saying prayers"; it may be likened to the attitude of a child who breaks into the presence of a mother saying: "I'll not say a word, if you will just let me stay here and watch you."

Meditation allows one to suspend the conscious fight against external diversions by an internal realization of the presence of God. It shuts out the world to let in the Spirit. It surrenders our own will to the impetus of the divine will. It turns the searchlight of divine truth on the way we think, act, and speak, penetrating beneath the layers of our self-deceit and egotism. It summons us before the bar of divine justice, so that we may see ourselves as we really are, and not as we like to think we are. It silences the ego with its clamorous demands, in order that it may hear the wishes of the divine heart. It uses our faculties, not to speculate on matters remote from God, but to stir up our will to conform more perfectly with His will. It cultivates a truly scientific attitude toward God as truth, freeing us from our prepossessions and our biases so that we may eliminate all wishful thinking from our minds.

It eliminates from our lives the things that would hinder union with God and strengthens our desire that all the good things we do shall be done for His honor and glory. It takes our eyes off the flux and change of life and reminds us of our *being*, the creatureliness, the dependence of all things on God for creation, moment-to-moment existence, and salvation. Meditation is not a petition, a way of using God, or asking things from God, but rather a surrender, a plea to God that He use us.

For meditation the ear of the soul is more important than the tongue: St. Paul tells us that faith comes from listening. Most people commit the same mistake with God that they do with their friends: They do all the talking. Our Lord warned against those who "heap up empty phrases, as the Gentiles do, for they think they will be heard because of their many words" (Mt 6:7). One can be impolite to God, too, by absorbing all the conversation, and by changing the words of Scripture from "Speak, Lord, Thy servant hears" to "Listen, Lord, Thy servant speaks." God has things to tell us that will enlighten us — we must wait for Him to speak. No one would rush into a physician's office, rattle off all the symptoms, and then dash away without waiting for a diagnosis; no one would tune in the radio and immediately leave the room. It is every bit as stupid to ring God's doorbell and then run away. The Lord hears us more readily than we suspect; it is our listening to God that needs to be improved. When people complain that their prayers are not heard by God, what often has happened is that they did not wait to hear God's answer. . . .

*   *   *

Meditation improves our behavior. It is often stated that it makes no difference what we believe, that it all depends on how we act; but this is meaningless, for we act upon our beliefs. Hitler acted on the theory of Nazism and produced a war; Stalin acted on the ideology of Marx and Lenin and begot slavery. If our thoughts are bad, our actions will also be bad. The problem of impure actions is basically the problem of impure thoughts; the way to keep someone from robbing a bank is to distract that person from thinking about robbing a bank. Political, social, and economic injustices are, first, psychic evils — they originate in the mind. They become social evils because of the intensity of the thought that begot them.

Nothing ever happens in the world that does not first happen inside a mind. Hygiene is no cure for immorality, but if the wellsprings of thought were kept clean, there would be no need to care for the effects of evil thinking on the body. When one meditates and fills the mind for an hour a day with thoughts and resolutions bearing on the love of God and neighbor above all things, there is a gradual seep-age of love down to the level of what is called the subconscious, and finally these good thoughts emerge, of themselves, in the form of ef-fortless good actions. Everyone has verified in his own life a thousand times the ideomotor character of thought. Watching a football game, the spectator sees a player running with the ball; if there is a beautiful opening around right end, he may twist and turn his own body more than the runner does, to try to take advantage of the chance. The idea is so strong that it influences his bodily movements — as ideas often do. Thoughts of fear produce "goose-pimples" and sometimes make the blood rush to the hands and feet. God has made us so that, when we are afraid, we should either fight or run.

Our thoughts make our desires, and our desires are the sculptors of our days. The dominant desire is the predominant destiny. Desires are formed in our thoughts and meditations; and since action follows the lead of desires, the soul, as it becomes flooded with divine promptings, becomes less and less a prey to the suggestions of the world.

If a person meditates consistently on God, a complete revolution takes place in that person's behavior. If in a morning meditation we remember how God became a humble servant of us, we will not lord it over others during the day. If there were a meditation of His redemp-tion of all people, we would cease to be snobs. Since Our Lord took the world's sins upon Himself, anyone who has dwelt on this truth will seek to take up the burdens of his or her neighbor, even though these bur-dens were not of the meditator's making — for the sins the Lord bore were not of His making, either. If the meditation stressed the merciful Savior Who forgave those who crucified Him, so we will forgive those who injure us, that we may be worthy of forgiveness. These thoughts do not come from ourselves — for we are incapable of them — nor from the world — for they are unworldly thoughts. They come from God alone.

Once our helplessness is rendered up to the power of God, life changes, and we become less and less the victims of our moods. In-stead of letting the world determine our state of mind, we determine the state of soul with which the world is to be faced. The earth carries its own atmosphere with it as it revolves about the sun; so the soul can carry the atmosphere of God with it, in disregard of turbulent events in the world outside.

There is a moment in every good meditation when the God-life enters our life, and another moment when our life enters the God-life. These events transform us utterly. Sick, nervous, fearful people are made well by this communion of creature with creator, this letting of God into the soul. A distinguished psychiatrist, J. D. Hadfield, has said: "I attempted to cure a nervous patient with suggestions of quiet and confidence, but without success, until I had linked these suggestions on to that faith in the power of God which is the substance of the Christian's confidence and hope. Then the patient became strong."

It is never true to say that we have no time to meditate; the less one thinks of God, the less time there will always be for God. The time we have for anything depends on how much we value it. Thinking determines the uses of time; time does not rule over thinking. The problem of spirituality is never, then, a question of time; it is a problem of thought. For it does not require much time to make us saints; it requires only much love.

[Go to Heaven]

Angels

MANY PEOPLE, having seen my "angel" clean my blackboard on television, will ask on meeting me, "How is your angel?" So, let us talk about angels and their role in our lives. But here we use the word angel in a very restricted sense — not as a spiritual invisible messenger, not a special illumination or a winged creature bearing a summons, not even as a vision or anything preternatural. By an angel we mean here any person or event that has changed the whole course of our life, influenced our behavior, made us turn right when we were about to turn left, and in general made us better. What lifts such a concept out of the natural order is that sooner or later it is seen as being an act of God.

Take, for instance, the story of young Tobias, who was sent by his father Tobit to the land of Media on a kind of economic mission. His mother was worried about sending the son on such a long journey, so she went out and found a guide, whose name was Raphael. Raphael not only protected Tobias from dangers and helped him to collect a debt, but even found a good wife for him. The Book of Tobias says, "Raphael was an angel, but he knew it not."

God sets many angels in our paths, but often we know them not; in fact, we may go through life never knowing that they were agents or messengers of God to lead us on to virtue, or to deter us from vice. But they symbolize that constant and benign intervention of God in human history, which stops us on the path to destruction or leads us to success or happiness and virtue.

God is generally operating behind secondary causes, like an anonymous benefactor. God's direction of our lives is so hidden that most of us are unaware of how we were made an angel to help a neighbor, or how a neighbor was made an angel for us. When I finished college, I took an examination for a national scholarship worth several thousand dollars. I was anxious to complete my education by working for a Ph.D., but at the same time, ever since my earliest recollection, I had wanted to be a priest. Accepting the university scholarship would have meant postponing my call to the priesthood and maybe endangering it. During the summer vacation after college graduation, I visited our professor of philosophy and told him with great glee that I had won the university scholarship. He grabbed me by the shoulders and said, "Do you believe in God?" I told him the question was silly. But he challenged me, "But do you believe in God practically?" When I answered in the affirmative he said, "You know your duty. Go to the seminary now and begin studies for the priesthood. Tear up the scholarship."

But I protested, "Why cannot I work now for my Ph.D. and then go later to the seminary?"

He retorted, "If you make that sacrifice, I promise you that after your ordination to the priesthood you will receive a far better university education than before." I tore up the scholarship, followed my duty, and after ordination as a priest, I spent almost five years in graduate studies — most of them in some of the great universities of Europe. The professor was my angel. I saw it then, but I see it more clearly now.

Dr. Paul Tournier, who is one of the greatest of modern psychiatrists, says that for years his life was banal and confused, and never entrusted clearly to the guidance of God. Both he and his wife made such a commitment to divine guidance and found great happiness. As he put it in one of his books, "God led us step by step, from event to event. Only afterwards, as we look back over the way we have come and reconsider certain important moments in our lives in the light of what followed them, or when we survey the whole progress of our lives, do we experience the feeling of having been led without knowing it, the feeling that God has mysteriously guided us. We did not perhaps know it at the time. Time had to elapse to enable us to see it. But He opened the unexpected horizon to us."

Francis Thompson, speaking of the universality of this kind of angel, said, "Stir but a stone and start a wing." They are everywhere — good angels — only we do not recognize them as such. But the tragedy is that there are sometimes bad angels — they are evil persons who pull us down to vice. The world is a battlefield of angels.

[Guide to Contentment]

Divinity is always where you least expect to find it.
[The Moral Universe]

Making Up
for Wasted Time

N EAR WHERE I LIVE, there is a small park just off a main
street. The other afternoon I saw five men spend about
three hours there playing cards. They were city workers
whose business it was to fix the potholes in the streets of New York.
This "goofing off" from work was wasting the taxpayers' money. The
scene evoked many thoughts concerning the pricelessness of time.

An ancient Persian proverb says that there are three things that
never return: the spent arrow, the spoken word, and the lost opportunity. No less impressive is the proverb of the sleepy African: "The
dawn does not come twice to waken a man." Browning expressed it
this way: "Youth once gone, is gone. Deeds, let escape, are never to be
done ... Nature has time, may mend mistakes, she knows occasion may
recur ... I must perish once and perish utterly."

According to a familiar Korean legend, a Sibyl came to the palace
of Tarquin II bearing nine volumes for which she demanded a high
price. Her offer being declined, she went away and burned three of the
volumes. Returning, she offered the six, but demanded the same price
as for the original nine. Again her proposal was rejected, and again she
departed and committed three more volumes to the flames. Once more
she returned, bearing the last three while demanding the same price as

for the nine. Tarquin bought the three, but the chance of ever seeing the nine books of "Sibylline verses" was forever lost.

Each moment wasted means that life's precious treasures are diminished while the price for them becomes higher. Opportunities both rise in price and grow fewer every time we refuse to make use of them. The passions and bad habits we refuse to tame today will be harder to conquer tomorrow should we leave the hours of today unimproved. Time forges new links and the slavery becomes more harsh. It is easy to acquire a talent for foreign languages and music when young, but difficult later on in life.

Time opens opportunities. When Moses led his people out of Egypt, God spoke to him: "You have been going about this mountain country long enough: turn northward." The time of probation was paid; the time of opportunity had come. The emancipation of slaves waited for Lincoln; the open door of Ephesus for Paul. As Shakespeare put it: "There is a tide in the affairs of men which, taken at the flood, leads on to fortune; omitted, all the voyage of their life is bound in shallows and in miseries."

Though time is too precious to waste, it must never be thought that what was lost is irretrievable. Once the Divine is introduced, then comes the opportunity to make up for losses. God is the God of the second chance. Peter denied, but he had the second chance in which to become as solid as a rock. Jonah, who refused to accept a mission, was given the second chance and saved Babylon. There really is such a thing as a "second birth." Being born again means that all that went before is not held against us. The thief on the right side of the Lord on Calvary wasted a human life, but in accepting pardon won eternal life.

Speaking to a group of young drug addicts once, I asked how many of them thought they were "hooked." Almost all hands went up. For them time held no promise but slavery to drugs. I took a rubber ball and rolled it down the middle aisle of the hall. Naturally, it went in a straight line. They all agreed it was a picture of their hopelessness. Time would not change them, but only deepen their addiction. Then I rolled the ball again down the aisle, and asked one of them to put out his foot in front of the ball. Immediately, the ball changed direction. So slavery to drugs would continue in a straight line of time unless a superior force intervened to alter its movement. So it is with grace or the extra power that comes from God when we ask for it. No wasted life need be final. We may close the door on opportunity, but divinity is still on the other side knocking, His hands full of gifts.

[On Being Human]

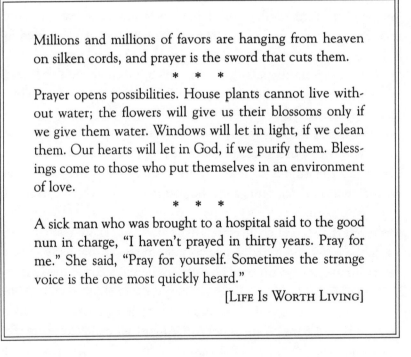

Millions and millions of favors are hanging from heaven on silken cords, and prayer is the sword that cuts them.

*   *   *

Prayer opens possibilities. House plants cannot live without water; the flowers will give us their blossoms only if we give them water. Windows will let in light, if we clean them. Our hearts will let in God, if we purify them. Blessings come to those who put themselves in an environment of love.

*   *   *

A sick man who was brought to a hospital said to the good nun in charge, "I haven't prayed in thirty years. Pray for me." She said, "Pray for yourself. Sometimes the strange voice is the one most quickly heard."

[Life Is Worth Living]

Peace

THE MESSAGE of the angels of Christmas was "on earth peace." What is peace? Peace is the tranquillity of order. It is not just tranquillity alone, for thieves can be tranquil in the possession of their spoils. Order or justice is the due subordination of parts to whole, of body to soul, and of humanity to God. Without order there can be no true tranquillity, which is peace.

The Christmas gift of peace was the uncoiling of the links of a triple chain that first unites a person with God, then with himself, and then with his neighbor.

*   *   *

One reason why we do not find peace is that we want to be saved but not from our vices, or because we want to be saved but at not too great a cost, or because we want to be saved in our way and not God's way. We miss peace because in each and every one of us there is a little secret garden that we keep locked. It contains the one thing we will not give up to have true peace of soul. The Christmas secret of peace is giving this secret garden and our whole human nature to God, as Mary gave Christ His human nature. Christmas reminds us that the reason we are not as happy as saints is because we do not wish to be saints.

*   *   *

To the descendants of the shepherds and the wise men, to the souls that still have roots, to all people of good will, whether they be Jew, Protestant, or Catholic, atheists, pagans, or enemies, the plea goes out to seek the Truth even though it be found in a place you presently believe to be as repugnant as a stable. That Babe came to earth at a time when the social order was most ripe for class war. There was conflict between Jew and Gentile; Samaritan and Jew; Roman and Greek; Scribe and Pharisee; "haves" and "have-nots"; dictators and oppressed; Caesars and anti-Caesars. And yet instead of capitalizing on any one class to win support, He chose the hard way — by preaching the unity of all people, first in Adam, then regenerated in Him, living in concord and peace through the charity of His Holy Spirit.

[REJOICE!]

We are related to our fellow man in the world as the cells of the body are related one to another. The good of one cell or the good of one organ is the good of the whole. . . . If a speck gets in the eye, the hand comes to its rescue. If one foot is hurt, the other foot does double duty. If the face is burned, the doctors will graft skin from another part of the body to restore the disfigured visage. If a patient is suffering from anemia, doctors will transfuse blood from one member of society to another to help that weakened blood condition. . . .

Applying the principle of solidarity in the spiritual order, it is possible to apply the merits of one person to another. If it is possible to graft skin, it is also possible to graft prayer. If it is possible to transfuse blood, it is also possible to transfuse sacrifice. There has been many a soul brought to God through the offered sufferings of others. . . .

[LIFE IS WORTH LIVING]

endowed with this sense of the invisible, the power of *seeing
ugh things,* and such is the essence of humor. . . .

* * *

n the gutter of a city street was a drop of water, dirty and stag-
'ay up in the heavens a gentle sunbeam saw it, leaped out of its
y, down to the drop, kissed it, thrilled it through and through
w strange life and hope, and lifted it up higher and higher and
beyond the clouds, and one day let it fall as a flake of im-
e snow on a mountaintop. And so our own lives — humdrum,
tiresome lives of a workaday world — can be ennobled, spiritu-
nd sacramentalized, provided we bring to them the inspiration
One who saw apostolic zeal in salt, provided we infuse their
blackness with the electric flame of love that will make them
th the brilliance of a diamond, provided we bring to them the
on of the great Captain who carries five wounds in the fore-
battle, and thrills them with the fixed flash of the lightning
ternal as the Light.

when we have done this, then perhaps we will understand why
o came to this earth to teach us the divine sense of humor
us everything that was lovely and beautiful in His character —
ne thing. He showed us His power; He showed us His wisdom;
wed us His melting kindness; He showed us His sorrow; He
us His tears; He showed us His forgiveness; He showed us His
ver nature; He showed us His knowledge of human hearts.

here was one thing that He did not show; there was one thing
d for those who do not take this world too seriously; there was
ng He saved for paradise; there was one thing He saved for
ho, like poets and saints, have a divine sense of humor; there
thing He saved for heaven that will make heaven heaven —
t was His smile!

[Moods and Truths]

The Divine
of Hum

ALMIGHTY GOD willed that just as
make us think of the artist, and ev
remind us of the architect who de
in this world should, in some way, remind
God made the world with a *Divine Sense of*

Do we not say that a person has a sens
through things," and do we not say that
humor if he cannot "see through things"?
according to such a plan that we were const
things" to Him, the power, the wisdom, t
of all that is. In other words, the material
the spiritual, the human the revelation of t
the passing, the revelation of the Eternal.
God's original plan, was transparent, like a
ing to that plan a mountain was not just a
the revelation of the power of God. A suns
sunset was the revelation of the beauty of
just a snowflake; a snowflake was the revel
Everything told us something about God, f
the world is the power and wisdom of the
ifest. According to this plan, every one wa

who is
God th

Down
nant.
azure s
with n
higher,
macul
routine
alized,
of Son
carbon
glow w
inspira
front c
made

And
He W
showed
except
He sh
showed
power

But
He sa
one th
those
was or
and th

Sources

Cross-Ways. Garden City, N.Y.: Doubleday/Image, 1984.

Footprints in a Darkened Forest. New York: Meredith Press, 1967.

Go to Heaven. New York: McGraw-Hill Book Company, Inc., 1960.

God and War. New York: P. J. Kenedy and Sons, 1943.

Guide to Contentment. New York: Simon and Schuster, 1967.

Life Is Worth Living. First Series. New York: McGraw-Hill Book Company, Inc., 1953.

Life Is Worth Living. Second Series. New York: McGraw-Hill Book Company, Inc., 1954.

Life Is Worth Living. Third Series. New York: McGraw-Hill Book Company, Inc., 1955.

Life Is Worth Living. Fourth Series. New York: McGraw-Hill Book Company, Inc., 1956.

Life Is Worth Living. Fifth Series. New York: McGraw-Hill Book Company, Inc., 1957.

Life of Christ. New York: McGraw-Hill Book Company, Inc., 1958; Doubleday, 1977.

Lift Up Your Heart. New York: McGraw-Hill Book Company, Inc., 1950.

Love, Marriage and Children. New York: Dell Publishing, Co., Inc., 1963.

Moods and Truths. New York: The Century Co., 1932. Reprinted in 1950 by Garden City Publishing Co., Garden City, New York.

Old Errors and New Labels. New York: The Century Co., 1931. Reprinted in 1950 by Garden City Publishing Co., Garden City, New York.

On Being Human. Garden City, N.Y.: Doubleday & Co., 1982.

Peace of Soul. New York: McGraw-Hill Book Company, Inc., 1949.

Philosophy of Religion: The Impact of Modern Knowledge on Religion. New York: Appleton-Century-Crofts, Inc., 1948.

Preface to Religion. New York: P. J. Kenedy & Sons, 1946.

Rejoice! Garden City, N.Y.: Doubleday/Image, 1989.

The Divine Romance. New York: The Century Co., 1930; New York: Alba House, 1986.

The Eternal Galilean. New York: D. Appleton-Century Company, Inc., 1934. Reprinted in 1950 by Garden City Books, Garden City, New York.

The Hymn of the Conquered. Huntington, Ind.: Our Sunday Visitor, 1933.

The Life of All Living: The Philosophy of Life. New York: The Century Company, Inc., 1929. Reprinted in 1951 by Garden City Books, Garden City, New York.

The Moral Universe: A Preface to Christian Living. Milwaukee: The Bruce Publishing Company, 1936.

The Power of Love. New York: Simon and Schuster, 1965.

The World's First Love. New York: McGraw-Hill Book Company, Inc., 1952.

Those Mysterious Priests. Garden City, N.Y.: Doubleday & Company, Inc., 1974.

Thoughts for Daily Living. Garden City, N.Y.: Doubleday, 1955.

Three to Get Married. New York: Appleton-Century-Crofts, Inc., 1951.

Treasure in Clay. Garden City, N.Y.: Doubleday/Image, 1982; San Francisco: Ignatius Press, 1993.

Way to Happiness. New York: Garden City Books, 1954.

What Good Am I Doing Here? New York: The Society for the Propagation of the Faith, n.d.

Fulton J. Sheen

FULTON J. SHEEN (1895–1979) was perhaps this century's most widely acclaimed and best-loved Roman Catholic prelate. A participant in the Second Vatican Council, he was Titular Archbishop of Newport and national director of the World Mission Society for the Propagation of the Faith.

Bishop Sheen was also an influential master of the media with a far-ranging impact on our culture. The first regular speaker on NBC-Radio's Sunday evening *Catholic Hour,* he received as many as six thousand letters a day from listeners, about a third of them non-Catholics, and millions of his radio talks were distributed in the United States alone. A pioneer in television when the medium was just gaining popularity, he hosted the enormously popular series *Life Is Worth Living* from 1951 to 1957 as well as three subsequent TV series. Chaplain of the Catholic Actors Guild, he received an Emmy Award in 1952, three successive Look Television Awards, and, in 1968, the coveted Catholic Radio and Television Association Award.

A gifted professor of philosophy at Catholic University in the 1920's, Bishop Sheen held a J.C.B. degree from that institution, as well as a Ph.D. from the University of Louvain, Belgium, which later awarded him the Cardinal Mercier International Philosophy Award. He also attended the Sorbonne in Paris and received an S.T.D. from Collegio Angelico in Rome. A spiritual master and teacher of the first order, Bishop Sheen achieved international recognition for his scores of bestselling books, syndicated columns, and worldwide lecture appearances.